CARING COUPLES
NETWORK
HANDBOOK

RICHARD & JOAN HUNT

DISCIPLESHIP RESOURCES
MATERIALS FOR GROWTH IN CHRISTIAN FAITH & LIFE
— NASHVILLE, TENNESSEE —

P.O. Box 840 • Nashville, TN 37202 • Phone (615) 340-7068

Scripture quotations, unless otherwise indicated, are from the New Revised Standard Version of the Bible, copyright © 1989 by the Division of Christian Education of the National Council of Churches of Christ in the United States of America, and are used by permission. All rights reserved.

ISBN 0-88177-193-7

Library of Congress Catalog Card No. 96-85807

DR193

TABLE OF CONTENTS

Introduction

Introducing the Caring Couples Network

The Caring Couples Network is couples helping other couples in cooperation with pastors. The Caring Couples Network brings together many resources to focus on many ministries with, to, and for couples and families. The following answers to common questions about this exciting ministry will acquaint you with some basic concepts and terms.

What Is the Caring Couples Network?

The Caring Couples Network brings together healthy married couples in a covenant to support other couples who want to grow in marriage and family relationships. Couples in the network provide support by committing to relationships of care and by creating strategies to meet marital and family needs.

The purpose of the network is to encourage couples to strengthen their commitment to each other in love by providing support at transitional stages of family life and in marital crises.

The Caring Couples Network is a ministry of the church. This comprehensive, integrated, couple-to-couple approach seeks to enable people to experience God's love in order to better express love to their spouses. Pastors play an essential role in leading this ministry.

This ministry is a network. The network connects teams of couples with other caregivers, resources, and church structures in order to meet the needs of couples and families. The Caring Couples Network builds teams of people with deliberate strategies to encourage healthy, growing Christian marriages.

What Is a Caring Couple?

Central to the concept of a caring network is the caring couple. Caring Couples are married partners in healthy, growing marriages who covenant with God and the church to minister with couples in need. Committed Christian couples are the key to encouraging spiritual, emotional, and relational health in other couples. Chapter 3 provides additional information about the characteristics and responsibilities of Caring Couples.

What Is a Partner Couple?

The term used in this handbook to refer to those who receive care from caring couples is "Partner Couple." Partner Couples need to be open to receiving the nurture of Caring Couples. The term "Partner Couple" is used to indicate that relationships often involve mutual ministry among couples. Partner Couples include both couples facing chronic instability and couples in transitional stages (for instance, engaged and newly married couples, couples at the birth of a child, families with adolescent children, empty nest families).

What Is a Caring Couples Network Team?

Caring Couples team with pastoral leaders and professional consultants to form the Caring Couples Network. Together the couples form the local Caring Couples Network Team. The team develops a strategic plan tailored to meet local needs with the available resources. The team supports caring couples in their own marriages and in their ministries with other couples. Chapter 4 outlines the organization of the local Caring Couples Network Team.

What Is the Goal of the Caring Couples Network?

The goal of the Caring Couples Network is to develop Christian couples by creating and training an intentional group of Caring Couples who minister with couples and families. The network seeks to connect Caring Couples to resources for nurturing healthy relationships within the marriage partnership. The purpose of the network is to encourage the health of marriages in order to improve the quality of living for spouses and children.

How Does the Caring Couples Network Team Help the Pastor's Marriage and Family Counseling Ministry?

The Caring Couples Network supports and extends the pastor's counseling in many ways but does not replace the pastoral care and counseling to which pastors are called.

Why Does the Caring Couples Network Focus on Married Couples?

The network emphasizes married couples because the wife-husband relationship is grounded in the covenant they make before God and the community to live together as spouses. The spousal relationship directly impacts the health of all relationships in the family. The wedding upholds this covenant as the basis for family values and healthy relationships. Committed Christian couples shape family values and provide real-life examples that demonstrate God's intentions for families.

Is the Caring Couples Network Limited to Caring for Married Couples?

The larger purpose of the Caring Couples Network is to build the interpersonal relationships of all couples so they will provide leadership for healthy homes. The Caring Couples Network's concern for married couples also suggests additional ministries with single-parent families. Chapter 13 describes ways to minister to unmarried couples, single parents, and other individuals who are not married.

How Can the Reader Best Use this Handbook?

This handbook introduces the Caring Couples Network. The *Caring Couples Network Handbook* offers many suggestions, perspectives, and resources. We know that each ministry context is unique. We encourage you to adapt these ideas to your unique setting. The handbook will often outline a specific model or method. You should view these as suggestions which can be modified to meet needs in the church or community where you live.

For the sake of brevity, the handbook will generally speak of the pastor as if she or he were married and leading a congregation in a single-charge assignment without additional pastoral staff. Although this set of circumstances may describe the situation for the majority of those who use this handbook, the handbook is not limited to such situations. Churches with unmarried pastors as well as those with multiple staff members will benefit as much from the handbook as those typically described. Large churches may multiply the structures suggested in the pages that follow. Smaller churches may cooperate with other churches to provide these caring ministries. All who use the book should feel free to modify the suggestions to meet the needs in their own settings.

The Caring Couples Network can be ecumenical. All churches need a Caring Couples Network Team. We have prepared the Caring Couples Network materials so any Christian group may adapt them and use them in their context. We expect Caring Couples to discover other ways of nurturing couples. Caring Couples may share their experiences with other Caring Couples in their community.

The *Caring Couples Network Handbook* is a tool to connect all United Methodist Church publications, resources, and couples in ministries that support healthy marriages and families. Each chapter in this handbook offers many possibilities for ministry and points to additional resources.

Chapters 1–5 provide an overview of the Caring Couples Network. Chapters 1–2 offer basic theological bases for the Caring Couples Network vision for marriage ministries. Chapter 3 identifies the qualities of Caring Couples. Chapter 4 describes Caring Couples Network Team organization. Developing a local plan for action is essential to the success of the network.

Chapters 6–9 list resources available for marriage enrichment.

Chapters 10–13 suggest ministries to meet specific situations, including premarital and early marriage stages, parenting, dysfunctional families, single parent families, and singles.

Chapters 14–17 describe how the Caring Couples Network connects to existing resources of the church, community, and denomination. Chapter 18 outlines the development of a community marriage policy. Chapter 19 brings an overall perspective to the ministry of the Caring Couples Network.

Chapter 1
The Caring Couples Network Vision for Nurturing Healthy Marriages

The Spirit of the Caring Couples Network

The Caring Couples Network supports couples who profess faith in God and who covenant to grow in love in their relationship with each other. God intends marriage to express the relatedness of humans to God. As spouses experience God's grace, they are better able to express love to their partner in Christ.

Commitment to God and to spouse is essential to building a marriage in the context of God's love. As couples pray and listen, the Holy Spirit gives love in their hearts, words in their mouths, and faithfulness in their living. Caring Couples find joy, courage, and hope in God's presence, guidance, and nurture.

The Dynamic Basis of the Caring Couples Network

At the heart of the Caring Couples Network are married couples who care for each other and who together care about others. The Caring Couples Network is couples helping other couples in cooperation with the pastor and in consultation with professionals from many disciplines. Each local Caring Couples Network Team has access to other Caring Couples Network Teams, as well as to many resources that can strengthen Christian couples and families.

The essence of the Caring Couples Network is the interpersonal relationship of Caring Couples with Partner Couples. All resources are intended to support this central personal relationship.

The network of Caring Couples seeks to embody Christ's Spirit for couples to experience. The Caring Couples movement encourages growth in healthy marriages between persons of faith. Healthy marriages are grounded in God's purpose in Jesus Christ—to bring people together in loving commitment. Marriage unites women and men as co-equals before God. The many biblical bases for the ministries of the Caring Couples Network are described in Chapter 2.

God's Call to a Ministry of Reconciliation

Christians are called to a reconciliation ministry (2 Corinthians 5:17–6:2). Couples follow the leading of the Holy Spirit as they create their own marriage style through discussion, negotiation, and practice with feedback. God calls every couple to constant renewal of love every day. Forgiveness is the "reset button" to open additional ways to care for each other. Jesus teaches that anyone who provides any ministry that accomplishes healing and reconciliation with God is welcome and valued by God.

Caring Couples are committed to examine all claims, agencies, policies, and models concerning families to see whether they accomplish healing and reconciliation. Any couple who seeks to advance the Caring Couples Network goals and qualities is welcome as part of the Caring Couples Network. The Caring Couples Network welcomes a variety of programs and resources in order to meet the needs of different situations, couples, and families.

Galatians 6:2–5 teaches both mutual and individual responsibility. The networks of friends, families, and congregation commit themselves to encourage, support, and nurture every marriage. Since the church wants couples to succeed in love, the church needs to help them to grow in love.

God's Call to a Ministry in Partnership

According to Luke 10:1–2 Jesus sent out workers two by two.

Today the Caring Couples Network also calls persons "two by two" in the form of a married couple sent out to minister in the name of Christ.

Matthew 18:19–20 promises Christ's presence when two or three are gathered in his name. In Ecclesiastes 4:9–12 the advantage of two partners and the strength of a threefold cord are celebrated. Combinations of two persons (as in marriage) and three persons or groups with the same values and goals are powerful when working and acting together.

A Christian husband and wife are the "two" who live together in Christ's name. A husband and wife with God can be a secure triangle of peace and blessing to all. With God the spouses form a "threefold cord" that cannot be easily broken by any outside force. When three join, the result is tremendous strength. The Caring Couples Network Team with pastor, Caring Couples, and consultants may be seen as the "three," a strong "triangle" that supports loving marriages and families. The Caring Couples Network Team forms a "threefold cord" that is a strong lifeline to couples and families.

The Caring Couples Network Expresses Our Covenants

The covenants described in the *Service of Baptism* and the *Service of Christian Marriage* call the church to provide nurture to couples and families.

Our Commitment to Couples

The Service of Christian Marriage (*The United Methodist Hymnal,* 1989, pp. 864–869) invites the congregation of relatives and friends to support and nurture the married couple throughout their lives.

In the initial greeting the pastor reminds the people they "are gathered together in the sight of God to witness and bless the joining together" of the couple.

In the response of the families and people, the pastor asks all present, "Will all of you, by God's grace, do everything in your power to uphold and care for these two persons in their marriage?"

In the dismissal the pastor speaks the final words to the people present: "Bear witness to the love of God in this world, so that those to whom love is a stranger will find in you generous friends."

Our Commitment to Nurture Children and Others

A similar blessing, charge, and calling is contained in the service for baptismal covenant for children and others unable to answer for themselves. The service of baptism for children expresses the concern that Christians have for persons at every stage of life. The baptismal service expresses God's covenant with us and each person's response to live in this covenant. The congregation also renews their covenant to give support to persons receiving baptism.

In the baptism of infants and young children, parents, sponsors, and the congregation pledge themselves to care for these children. The Baptismal Covenant II (*The United Methodist Hymnal*, 1989, 39–43) illustrates the concern for each child and family.

Parents who present children for baptism are asked about their intent to "live before these children a life that becomes the Gospel . . . and keep these children under the ministry and guidance of the Church . . . ."

The congregation pledges to "so order our lives after the example of Christ that the children, surrounded by steadfast love, may be established in the faith and confirmed and strengthened in the way that leads to life eternal."

The pastor's prayer for the children asks God to "guide and uphold the parents/sponsors of these children that, by living care, wise counsel, and holy example, they may lead (these children) into that life of faith whose strength is righteousness and whose fruit is everlasting joy and peace . . . ."

The Caring Couples Network purpose is to share these blessings with couples and families at every stage of their marital journey and family development. Caring

Couples share God's blessings with other couples in many nurturing and supportive ways.

The Need for the Caring Couples Network Ministry

Most of the major problems in society, such as crime, violence, and drug abuse, are rooted in unhealthy family situations. (See, for example, McManus, *Marriage Savers,* especially chapters 1–3.) Marital distress causes depression and decreases productivity and physical health (Markman, Stanley, and Blumberg, *Fighting for Your Marriage,* 1–4). Depending on several factors, an average of half of all marriages eventually end in divorce (Gottman, *What Predicts Divorce?,* 1–3).

Marriage quality (satisfaction, happiness) is different than marital status (married, divorced). Many couples who continue in their marriage are distressed. Nearly all spouses disagree with each other, but those who are unable to work through disagreements miss important support, become more dissatisfied, and are much more likely to separate and divorce (Gottman, *What Predicts Divorce?,* Chapter 5).

Church attendance (i.e., the couple being actively involved in a church) is associated with lower divorce (Gottman, *What Predicts Divorce?,* Chapter 5). Churches can do much more to strengthen and support healthy marriages at every stage (McManus, *Marriage Savers,* Chapters 1–3).

The Caring Couples Network is a major answer to the crises and needs of families in every community.

Loving Couples:
The Key to Strong Families

The Caring Couples Network emphasizes married couples because the husband and wife share in leading the family. The nature of the couple's relationship shapes family life. Growing, healthy marriages are the key to the spiritual nurture of each family member.

Growing marriages enable the family to be the "church at home." The family becomes the seven-day-a-week spiritual formation laboratory for both children and parents. As spouses grow in love, they can nurture other members of the household.

The quality of marriage is the fundamental key to family health since the wife and husband are the leaders of the family. The couple acts as priests in the home by nurturing the faith of each family member (Thompson, *Family: The Forming Center*).

Parents have the power to shape the family atmosphere. In large measure, adults control values formation, especially respect for persons and property, self-identity, self-esteem, and related basic life dimensions. Personal character develops in the years of childhood and adolescence.

The Caring Couples Network emphasizes the primary importance of the couple's Christian faith. The couple's values and lifestyle impact children, work, leisure, education, health, and other areas of living. Marriage certainly invites two persons to learn to love each other; yet it is much more than this. The marriage relationship also affects the values parents give to their children, and the participation of families in churches, schools, neighborhoods, work-home interfaces, and intergenerational relationships.

Developing Individual
Responsibility in the Family

A major goal for Christian families is to learn to love each other as Christ loves them. The values of love, care, concern, and cooperation are rooted in the faith of the parents. Parents work together to lead their household toward clear values with flexible ways to achieve them. Spouses with clear goals and mutual cooperation demonstrate positive models that empower children to love others.

Under God, parents help each child grow in faith and responsibility according to age and developmental level. The parents' goal for the family is to maximize growth in all individual, family, and community relationships.

At every age family members can learn to talk together in safety and to make responsible choices. Since younger children need much more structure and guidance, parents need to make many decisions for their younger children. As children grow older, parents share more of the decision process. In this way parents gradually pass more decisions to their maturing children, modeling cooperation, love, and sharing.

All persons affected by a decision should have input and arrive at common decisions. Any member may propose changes. All members have an opportunity to express their viewpoints. Parents oversee this process so their adolescent children emerge as responsible adults. In these ways rules are guidelines for acting in love rather than externally imposed demands.

Bible study and family devotions led by each family member as appropriate to age help all become more aware of God's continuing presence. Caring Couples assist other couples to know God's grace at deep levels and be able to talk about anything.

Family members work together to extend friendship to others in the name of Christ.

Creating Solutions to the Crisis of the Family

The basic solution to the family crises in our society and in our churches is to support Christian marriages. Offering nurture to couples benefits families and offers an example of Christ's intention for families.

The Caring Couples Network is a major ministry response to the crises of the family. The Caring Couples Network Team links Caring Couples with partner couples.

The Potential for the Caring Couples Network

If we assume that even half of the forty-eight million married couples in the U.S. are happy and successful, some twenty-four million couples are potential Caring Couples. What a tremendous improvement among all families could be made if these healthy couples were actively reaching out to help other couples and families. Perhaps many of these are already helping other couples through friendships, work, and volunteer activities.

The United Methodist Church as a denomination probably has well over a million healthy couples who could minister to family issues. If even ten percent of these couples became involved in Caring Couples Network Teams, there would be some one hundred thousand couples offering ministries such as those described in this handbook. Each year hundreds of thousands of couples and families would greatly benefit from networking with these healthy couples through the Caring Couples Network.

The exact number of Caring Couples in a congregation may vary from one to many couples; yet, every congregation has couples who care and who can join in the ministries that the Caring Couples Network Teams can offer.

Chapter 2
Biblical Basis for the Caring Couples Network

The Caring Couples Network is designed to encourage couples to grow in healthy marriages centered in the Christian way. The biblical teachings about marriage and divorce as outlined in this chapter offer Caring Couples Network Teams basic principles for nurturing marriage growth in the church.

God's Creation Purpose for Women and Men

"God made them male and female . . . and the two shall become one . . ." (Mark 10:6–8).

God has lovingly created every person as male or female and calls each to grow in love as God's creation. Man and woman are equal before God, enabling both to walk together on equal terms. The equality of male and female is clearly reaffirmed in such passages as St. Paul's declaration: *"As many of you as were baptized into Christ have clothed yourselves with Christ. There is . . . no longer male and female; for all of you are one in Christ Jesus"* (Galatians 3:27–28).

In Mark 10 Jesus refers to the creation story in contrast to easy divorce (a practice based on one interpretation of Deuteronomy 24:1–4). Jesus attributed the breaking of the marriage vow (divorce) to the unwillingness of both spouses to cultivate love. This is the "hardness of heart" of **both** spouses that causes divorce.

Caring couples consciously choose to be "one flesh." They express this unity in their exchange of solemn vows, their affection for each other, their lifestyle, and their relationships with their extended families. "One flesh" suggests "one corporate body" with wife and husband as the two equal members. This includes both the unity of sexual intercourse and the couple's choice to be "of one accord" in their values, goals, and ways they live all aspects of their lives.

When a man and woman love each other deeply enough, they are proud to state their commitment in a public wedding service. The church responds with nurture, support, and education for marriage and family living.

In the wedding vows the wife and husband commit themselves to God and to each other. They promise to learn to live as a married unit. The spouses know this is awe-inspiring as well as difficult; yet, they trust God and others to support them. They seek to grow in love through their lifetime journeys together.

(Some material in this chapter is quoted and edited from *A Service of Christian Marriage [Supplemental Worship Resources #5;* Nashville: Abingdon, 1979] 13-18, and is used by permission.)

Guidelines for Family Living

"Be subject to one another out of reverence for Christ. Wives . . . to your husbands . . . Husbands, love your wives . . . Children, obey your parents . . . [Parents], do not provoke your children to anger, but bring them up in the discipline and instruction of the Lord" (Ephesians 5:21–6:4).

The house rules in Ephesians 5 characterize family relations as mutually submissive. Submission suggests mutual commitment, but not hierarchy. The husband-wife relationship takes priority. Together, parents exercise responsibility for child discipline.

Marriage is the basic bond that largely determines the quality of families, the basic meeting of man and woman, a laboratory for learning to love and care for each other and to reach out to all persons in Christ's name. As Christians we assume that the primary family structure consists of wife and husband and their children. The Christian wedding service with its marriage vows supports this concept.

All other variations of family (such as one-parent families, step-families, children's homes and agencies) result from the absence of a marriage bond between the woman and man who procreated the children. When one or both parents are not present in the home, other care must be provided by the church, relatives, foster parents, or other agencies. In these cases the Caring Couples Network may intervene to provide additional nurture.

Loving Neighbor as Oneself

In Mark 12:28–34 Jesus teaches all people about loving God, neighbor, and self. Each partner respects the spouse as a neighbor in Christ. First John 3:18 adds that love must go beyond "word or speech" to "truth and action."

Covenant Commitment

According to Genesis 8:20–9:17, God's covenants are everlasting and accompanied by symbols of promise. Christian marriage is a special covenant set in the context of God's covenant with us as human beings. The commitment and "solemn vow" to stay together as spouses sets Christian marriage apart from civil marriage and from living together without an intentional public marriage commitment. Christian marriage is indeed a challenge to grow in love across a lifetime of "better, worse, richer, poorer, sickness, and health."

Christian marriage is a sign of a lifelong covenant between a man and a woman. They fulfill each other, and their love enables each to grow in love for the other, for God, and for others. Out of this steadfast love they can create new persons, their children (by birth or adoption). God's first intention is that the security of the marriage bond also be the foundation for their children and household.

The union of love is possible when Christ becomes the bond of unity. When both spouses center their lives in God, Christ is the uniting bond. As Paul writes in Ephesians 5:21, the marriage relationship reflects commitment to Christ. Paul's whole discussion makes sense only in the light of that basic and mutual bond between each spouse and Christ. The marriage covenant, part of the greater covenant that God continues to make with all humans, grows out of the Christian bond.

Christian marriage confirms the grace-filled equality of female and male in Christ. The marriage of a believing couple is a covenant between equals that celebrates their unity in Jesus Christ. They become a family within the larger household of God. They become one flesh within the body of Christ. In Christian marriage God's creation pattern of female and male equality can become a reality.

The Sacramental Nature of Marriage

The Protestant Reformers of the sixteenth century were unwilling to call marriage a sacrament because they did not regard matrimony as a necessary means of grace for salvation. Although not necessary to salvation, certainly marriage is a means of grace, thus sacramental in character. It is a covenant grounded in God's love for all and in the creation of humans as male and female.

A Christian marriage is both a plea for, and an expression of, daily graces. The married couple's way of life is to be a sign of what the church ought to be: a safe and dependable community of God's love. The fidelity of spouses to God and to each other is the strongest indication we have that the Christian life is possible in our world. Nowhere else in society are adults so completely free to choose to love and so completely in control of how they will respond to each other.

Paul contended that marriage between a Christian and non-Christian is also a holy union and a means for conversion (1 Corinthians 7:14a). Being "Christian" or "non-Christian" involves both one's inner spirit (faith, intention, vow) and one's outer actions (behavior, habits, "works"). Since biblical times, both faith and work have been essential. Saying "I love you" to one's spouse means little if actions are not caring

and nurturing. Conversely, even caring actions mean little if they come out of a spirit of selfishness and manipulation. Both actions and attitudes need to express love. One does not replace the other.

God the Holy Spirit is willing to be present in every marriage. Every marriage, whether healthy or dysfunctional, is possible only because God calls us to choose life, yet requires that the consequences of our choices be experienced by many in the human community. As noted in Chapter 3, these issues arise in every aspect of the Caring Couples Network Team ministries.

Purposes of Marriage

In earlier generations the classic purposes of marriage were considered first to bear children, then to avoid (sexual) sin, and finally to enable companionship. Today most Christians would reverse this order.

To Be a Caring Community

The primary purpose of marriage is to enable the wife and husband to establish a home or "mutual society." The Christian community of the family is more than a private friendship; it is a relationship in and of the church as household of God, a "domestic church," stabilized by the commitment of each spouse to the other and of both spouses to Christ.

The Christian community of the family is more than a private friendship; it is a relationship of nurturing love that enables the family to carry out its duties and responsibilities in the Christian community for society at large. The church witnesses to God's justice and love in both private and public life. Christian families are members of the church and citizens of the state. The quality of Christian marriages and families should not only be as good as the best in secular society, but it should also be growing toward the greater love that God in Christ gives.

To Do Good Instead of Sin

The second purpose of marriage is to avoid sin. Our understanding of sin should not be limited to the narrow definition of sexual infidelity. More basically, sin is the deep desire of every person to be first, even ahead of God. In marriage, God teaches spouses not to put their own desires ahead of God or their mates.

Marriage is a laboratory for learning how to love in the fullest and deepest sense of the term. Sexual union is one expression of intimacy and love. Sex is a means of grace and self-giving in the marriage covenant. Sexual intimacy is God's gift to be accepted and enjoyed in marriage.

In marriage, spouses are called not merely to avoid evil, but to learn how to extend care in many ways. As a result, life-long growth "avoids sin." When they fail, spouses can forgive each other, renew their efforts to love, and accept nurture for growing in love for neighbor, especially spouses and other family members.

To Choose Concerning Children

Once spouses have established a caring home and are seeking to grow in love, they may be ready for the third purpose of marriage—to have children. While many couples at their weddings already have children and are deprived of this free choice concerning children, the Christian value is that

couples can choose whether, when, and how to have children.

Commitment in Marriage

The service of marriage celebrates the all-embracing good news of God's grace. Christian marriage is a covenant of grace which undergirds the state's civil contract. Promises and responsibilities in the services for Christian marriage are not merely legal contracts. These Christian promises go beyond the law. They are unconditional expectations of the couple. Given in their public vows, offered in Scripture and sermon, the promise of God's unconditional mercy and love enables the two persons to become one community.

Marriage makes explicit, real, and practical the spiritual commitment of the two spouses. Through marriage, Christians also celebrate a Christ who is against culture, of culture, above culture, in paradoxical relationship with culture, and transforming culture (H. Richard Niebuhr, *Christ and Culture*).

What about Divorce?

It is clear that God's intent for marriage is a life-long ("until death") covenant. A man and a woman commit to continue their marriage relationship and grow in love across all of life. Biblical teaching for life-long commitment and against divorce is found in Malachi 2:13–16; Matthew 5:31–32; 19:3–12; Mark 10:2–12; Luke 16:18; 1 Corinthians 7:10–16; Ephesians 5:21–33; Colossians 3:18–19; and Hebrews 13:4. Divorce is never a first choice, but occurs only after spouses have already madeother choices (Deuteronomy 24:1–4; Malachi 2:16).

We acknowledge the reality of divorce, but place it in the context of our Christian vision of marriage, grace and forgiveness, and renewal possibilities. Divorce may be seen from two different stages of marriage: pre-wedding and post-breakdown of marriage. Divorce is both an attitude (failure to work and grow together) and an outcome (what to do when all honest effort seems to fail).

The Pre-Wedding Perspective: No Divorce

The most basic reason for God's prohibition of divorce is that both the couple and the community will see marriage as the start of a lifelong journey for growth and development. Marriage is a commitment by both spouses from which there is no turning back. Assuming that divorce is an easy escape from the hard work of growing in relationship is disallowed in Christian marriage.

When partners enter marriage with thoughts of escape if the going gets too difficult, the "worse, poorer, and sickness" cycles will inevitably prompt them to seek the nearest exit. Perhaps every couple could find good reason to divorce. Committed couples use difficulties and disappointments as challenges to renewal, growth, constructive change, and obtaining help to do so.

From the pre-wedding perspective, every couple is to assume that they will remain committed to help each other grow in love. The support of Caring Couples and other friends and family is essential for lifelong commitment.

Mutual Joy Makes Divorce Unwanted

Most of the skills and ministries of Caring Couples Network Teams are for the purpose of enabling couples to learn how to increase their marriage enjoyment. When growing love makes it increasingly fun to be together, serious thoughts of divorce are crowded farther and farther out of mind. Communication, forgiveness, problem-solving, and renewal are essential in creating a marriage relationship that makes divorce unnecessary.

A major reason for the engaged and early-marriage Caring Couples Network ministry with couples is to enhance couple care, satisfaction, and enjoyment, which as a byproduct, also prevents divorce. Assuming an "absolutely no divorce" perspective at entry into marriage is necessary for spouses to become a unit and work toward common goals.

The Life Journey Perspective after Marriage Breakdown

In one sense divorce is never necessary if both spouses are fully committed to do whatever is necessary to grow and work with each other in marriage.

In some cases, however, the work necessary to accomplish essential growth and love is so great that it seems impossible for one or both spouses. When one spouse wants to work for the marriage but the other spouse wants out, the uncommitted spouse will usually force an end to the marriage. Marriage requires the free and complete commitment of both partners.

Since marriage is a dynamic system, it is vital to remember that, at an earlier point, both spouses freely entered the marriage and publicly stated a long-term commitment to grow in love. Along the journey something changed because of the actions of both spouses with each other. Thus, there is rarely if ever a fully "innocent" partner in a divorce. Whether aware or not, each partner has acted in ways that gradually pushed the other partner farther away until divorce seemed to be the only option.

Possible Contact Points

When spouses are considering divorce, it may be sobering to ask both spouses, "What did you do to get your spouse to leave you?" Each partner has contributed to the outcome of the marriage, so that neither can claim to be innocent.

In many situations, if a person had been as open and caring to the previous partner as he or she now is to a new partner, the previous marriage might have succeeded. Positive changes that a person may make in dress, attitude, and actions may come too late for the previous marriage, yet can now make the person more pleasant, attractive, and caring in the new marriage.

Forgiveness and Renewal

Just as forgiveness and renewal are essential for marriage to continue well, so forgiveness and renewal are essential in moving into divorce and in considering remarriage after a divorce. At many points

each couple must decide whether to continue together or to divorce. Our Christian perspective gives every couple this option because it is only through having real-life choices that each person can freely decide to continue in a marital journey with her or his spouse as partner.

Along the marriage journey, assuming that divorce is possible enables a couple to romanticize and renew their marriage. The possibility of divorce challenges each partner to grow or to face losing the partner in whom so much is invested. In this way divorce is not "cheap grace" but is a very serious alternative to be taken only when, after much help, it is clear that it is the less hurtful option.

Developing Your Perspectives

Each Caring Couples Network Team needs to explore these two perspectives and develop answers that they can then use in constructive ways with partner couples.

The majority of persons who divorce do enter into another marriage; they carry with them whatever previous marriage experiences they have had, including children, financial obligations, and emotional scars and reliefs. Caring Couples in which one or both partners were previously married can be especially valuable in helping the Caring Couples Network Team to discuss perspectives on marriage and divorce.

Chapter 3
Caring Couples Are . . .

Who Are Caring Couples?

Caring couples seek to be agents of peace, justice, equality, empowerment, faithfulness, and freedom for individuals, couples, and families.

As Caring Couples

We Are . . .	We Seek To . . .
Growing	Grow in love with God, each other, our families, and our neighbors.
Communicating	Communicate honestly in love.
Negotiating	Handle conflicts well and negotiate mutually beneficial goals.
Renewing	Deepen our commitment to our marriage covenant and to nurturing each other.
Learning	Regularly use the Bible, spiritual disciplines, and other resources to grow in our love for each other.
Reaching Out	Join in mutual support with other couples to help nurture other married couples and families.

Recognizing Essentials

It is difficult to put the essential qualities of caring couples into words, yet it is relatively easy to recognize a Caring Couple. The six key words to the left attempt to describe the essence of Caring Couples. What additional elements could be included in this list?

As Caring Couples we recognize that we have these qualities, yet always need to grow. We continually respond to the following five challenges in our marriages throughout the stages of our life journeys:

1. Future: Where Are We Going?

- We ask ourselves about our goals as a couple. Our aims include the desire to grow in love and to choose values and directions wisely.

2. Resources: What Resources Enable Us to Grow in Love?

- We take inventory of our skills, strengths, abilities, power, and networks in order to identify realistic possibilities.

3. Positives: How Are We Nurturing?

- We evaluate and seek to improve our expressions of love, finances, daily activities, work, and leisure.

4. Negatives: What Keeps Us from Growing?

- We appraise and seek to overcome our own dysfunctions, crises, and other hurts.

5. Connections: How Do We Connect These Qualities?

- We work to improve our ability to communicate with each other and to solve problems.

Expressions of These Qualities and Questions for Discussion

As a wife and husband who deeply care about others, especially their marriage and families, think together about couples and individuals who have made important contributions and influences in your own marriage. Among these you may remember . . .

- A person who encouraged her spouse to be fair to you and your spouse in supervisory decisions at work.
- A respected couple who supported efforts in your church and community to improve family life.
- A couple who have celebrated over fifty years of marriage and still enjoy each other and continue to encourage others.
- A couple who sponsored a couples or singles group and were always available to help with concerns.

- A person with whom you could talk about anything and who encouraged you in a worthwhile goal when it seemed that everything was against you.
- A pastor and spouse who actually lived many of the values you wanted for your own marriage.
- A group of couples in a church school class who shared their worries and dreams and supported each other in times of crisis.
- Prayer partners who have prayed for you, your marriage, and your family.
- Someone who lovingly stayed with his or her spouse through illness, yet describes blessings and joys in life.

Caring Couples experience support from others across their life journeys. In response, Caring Couples seek to encourage others. Caring Couples embody Christ's spirit of "love, joy, peace, patience, kindness, goodness, faithfulness, gentleness, self-control" (Galatians 5:22).

Each couple is unique and has something special about their marriage. This special relationship comes out of their vision of their own blessings and possibilities. Each couple has a unique story. Caring Couples tell their stories of giving and receiving. They describe difficulties, surprises, and joys. They speak of love and renewed faith.

Because of who they are, Caring Couples naturally seem to attract others and appear as genuine friends to others.

A Lively Vision of Marriage

A Caring Couple's vision for marriage guides them in their lifelong journey. Together they decide whether they are a couple that really cares. Others also make this evaluation of marriages. This evaluation process continues across a lifetime. Sometimes it may be overt and specific, but more often it is felt inwardly.

Questions for Discussion

Caring Couples can clarify their visions and values for their marriages by using these two steps. The questions may be considered either as a group or as individuals.

1. Together create a list of marriage values and goals that are important to you and your spouse in your own marriage. These may include communication, finances, conflict resolution, parenting, spirituality, sexual satisfaction, expressing affection, friendships with others, and the extended family.

2. For each category give yourselves one of three ratings:

(If your marriage is typically healthy, you will probably have some topics in each of these three rating categories.)

Work area. We need some help in this area. Even the most successful Caring Couple has some areas where they could use some help, encouragement, or additional ideas about their marriage and family living. Among these may be reminders about refreshing ways to show affection, additional information on financial matters, tips on parenting details, or new perspectives on handling conflicts or anger.

Strength. We are usually doing okay in this area. You probably rate many areas of your marriage at this level. This indicates that your marriage is positive and solid enough to keep you going at satisfying levels, perhaps with occasional ups and downs.

Mentor. We are able to help others in this area. Most Caring Couples have more areas in which they can mentor, help, and encourage other couples than they think.

Information and insights you gained because you coped with a crisis, conflict, loss, or unwanted change will be very helpful to others who are facing similar issues in their own marriage or family living.

Couples minister more effectively when they have clear values and goals, appropriate information, friendship skills for listening, encouragement, and knowledge of resources.

Caring Couples Are Seeking to Grow in Love

Caring Couples would be the first to say that they are not perfect. Many would probably be reluctant to see themselves as models for marriage. These couples agree with Paul in Philippians 3:13–14, where he emphasizes, "forgetting what lies behind and straining forward to what lies ahead, I press on toward the goal of the prize of the heavenly call of God in Christ Jesus."

Caring Couples know how to pick up the pieces when things go wrong. Caring Couples know that at times they fail to live their vision of joyful, exciting, loving marriages. They also know that their marriage relationship transforms their lives because they have experienced this renewal in many difficult times and have seen it work in their friends and relatives. They know how to turn to other couples, individuals, and professionals for renewed support, encouragement, and models.

Caring Couples seek to live in peace. The transforming power of God's love enables Caring Couples to cope well with difficult situations and learn new ways to love each other. Caring Couples regularly ask themselves, "What did we do well? How well do we listen? Are we open to the Holy Spirit and to each other? Can we discuss ideas and possibilities with each other with respect and openness?"

Couples Nurturing Couples

The Caring Couples Network emphasizes that in every couple spouses care about each other, yet they are still learning more about loving at every stage of life.

Couples who form the Caring Couples Network Team are in some way a bit further along in their journeys than the partner couples. Each couple learns from the other. Caring Couples Network Team couples are willing to try to share their experiences constructively with others who may benefit.

Caring Couples minister in many situations by providing positive modeling of strong Christian marriage. Ministries may be with couples who are engaged, newly married, new parents, and couples of any age, whether in the congregation or outside it. Any of these couples may need the caring couple's encouragement, models, and friendships to enable them to succeed in life.

Couples often face major crises or chronic problems. These may include alcoholism, abuse, extramarital affairs, loss of job, financial reverses, illness or death of a family member, chronic health conditions, or aging relatives. It is at any of these points of entry that caring couples engage in ministry.

Reaching Out to Couples Who Need Care: "Partner Couples"

The couples who receive care from caring couples are called Partner Couples. Partner Couples need to be open to receiving friendship, nurture, ministries, encouragement, and help with any of the issues identified above.

In couples' ministry a Caring Couple becomes a companion, mentor, and guide on behalf of the Caring Couples Network Team and the congregation. Caring Couples, in consultation with their pastor, may reach out to other couples through an invitation to a "two couple dinner out," an evening at a sports event or movie, and any other appropriate social contacts that help the couples develop rapport and build bridges for support.

The Caring Couple seeks to support the Partner Couple. The skills and resources of the Caring Couple and the needs of the Partner Couple determine the caring strategy. The Caring Couple may become an advocate for the Partner Couple, may help them make contact with available resources in the community, or may link them to others who are able to address their needs. The Caring Couple supports the Partner Couple as long as the care is needed. If a Partner Couple moves out of the area, the Caring Couple extends friendship by seeking to connect that couple to a Caring Couples Network Team in the couple's new location.

Ministries with Single Persons

Some teams may also minister to unmarried people, including those who have lost a spouse or partner through death, divorce, or desertion, or other situations where a couple relationship has been broken.

One advantage of having a Caring Couple reach out to non-couple situations is that those persons have the opportunity to observe how a married man and woman relate to each other. It also gives the individual an acceptable and safe way to relate to both genders. It models healthy couple dynamics for persons who either have seldom experienced these or who, as in the case of a spouse's death, had a good relationship that is now ended.

The aim of ministry to partner couples or individuals is to assist these adults to create loving, caring, and nurturing relationships for all the persons in the home.

Invitation to Caring Couples Network Ministry

The Caring Couples Network offers the opportunity to join with other couples in the ministry of building healthy marriages and families. The network can enable us to learn how to reach out to couples and families in need as well as to improve our own marriages.

Are you one of these Caring Couples?

Since you are reading this handbook, you already show that you do care about marriages and families. We invite you to read on and to take action now.

- If you are married, decide as a couple to reach out and encourage other couples beginning today. Use the Marriage Covenant Declaration on the next page to express your commitment.
- If you are a pastor, take steps now to establish a Caring Couples Network Team in your church.
- If you are a professional in any field concerning marriage and family matters, volunteer to consult with pastors and couples in a Caring Couples Network Team.
- If you are not in one of these categories but know others who are, urge them to support a Caring Couples Network Team in your area. If no team exists, urge them to start a Caring Couples Network Team now.

With every minute you wait, the marriage crisis grows worse. People's hurt increases. Because they hurt, they also hurt others. They need YOU now. You can help.

Marriage Covenant Declaration

As husband and wife we reaffirm our commitment to our covenant of marriage as follows:

We believe that God created man and woman, loves us, and wants us to grow in love, mutual satisfaction, and joy. God established the sanctity and companionship of marriage. God calls us to stay together for life so we both can learn how to love more completely.

We believe that as marriage partners we are accountable to God and to each other for the quality of our marriage. God calls us to love each other unconditionally, even on occasions when feelings of affection are not present. We renew our promise to love each other as an act of will until warm feelings return.

We believe that God calls us to be role models for our children, family, neighbors, and church, so we are open to God's guidance in nurturing these relationships.

Therefore, we now renew our vows of marital faithfulness and do promise before God and those we know that we will stay together in love, from this day forward, for better or worse, for richer or for poorer, in sickness and in health, to love and to cherish until we are parted by death.

We also pledge our commitment to strengthen and nourish the marriages of others and to establish Caring Couples Network Team ministries to marriages to help other couples to:

- Receive marriage preparation as engaged couples
- Strengthen existing marriages
- Cope with marriage difficulties
- Foster reconciliation between separated and divorced members.

We pledge to encourage our church to join with other congregations in a "Community Marriage Policy" to support healthy, satisfying marriages and reduce the divorce rate. For what God has joined together, let the church help hold together.

Pledge by:

_____

Husband

_____

Wife

Witnessed by:

_____

Pastor or Caring Couple

Date:

_____ day of _____, 19_____.

(This covenant is adapted from McManus, *Marriage Savers,* 329. See Chapter 19 for details of the Community Marriage Policy.)

Chapter 4
Organizing the Local Caring Couples Network Team

The church's commitment to encourage couples in their marriages and to nurture children in faith motivates the ministry of the Caring Couples Network. Organizing the local Caring Couples Network Team enables the church to bless couples and families in the name of Christ.

The Caring Couples Network Team can network with the local church's worship and church school ministries for children, youth, and adults to fulfill these commitments. Caring Couples Network Teams cooperate with lay ministries and lay counseling programs.

The Caring Couples Network Team takes the lead in implementing the ministries of the local church to all couples, both those in need and those who are doing well. The primary focus on couples is indicated by the unique influence couples have on the family.

The Caring Couples Network Team offers the channel that unites caring couples in the effort to support Christian marriages and families. The team depends on God to lead them as they organize to minister on behalf of God in Christ.

Caring Couples Network Team Sponsorship

Each local Caring Couples Network Team consists of couples who care enough to commit themselves to grow in their own marriages and to encourage other couples. Caring Couples Network couples organize themselves into one or more Caring Couples Network Teams sponsored by a local church or cluster of churches.

Although the Caring Couples Network originates in The United Methodist Church and with resources developed in United Methodist settings, the Caring Couples Network Team will function just as well as an ecumenical cooperative team among local churches of several denominations. Creative use of this handbook will enable Caring Couples Network Teams to organize in the way that best fits the local situation.

- *In a small-membership church,* one or two caring couples are enough to start a Caring Couples Network Team. They may also join with other congregations to form a larger network.
- *A large-membership church or several churches* may form more than one Caring Couples Network Team, with each team specializing for ministry. The several Caring Couples Network

Teams may work separately on detailed plans and cooperatively on common interests. Churches with several couples' classes or groups may have each form a Caring Couples Network Team.

- *Ecumenical* Caring Couples Network Teams may need to modify some terms and structure to reflect their community situations as they minister to couples and families. This Christian ministry transcends differences among Christian groups.

Through the Caring Couples Network Team, each Caring Couple cooperates with their pastor or team leader and works with a professional consultant. The Caring Couples Network links couples who are committed to support spiritual growth, family health, and marriage success. The Caring Couples Network embodies the church's concern to improve family life in the church and society.

Ministries to couples are especially needed at transitional crises in a couple's lifetime journey. The Caring Couples Network Team ministers to couples across the full range of major life transitions, celebrations, and crises. Chapter 4 outlines some of these, and they are discussed in greater detail in Chapter 10–13.

One initial task of the Caring Couples Network Team is to develop a plan of action. The team will survey the wide range of possible ministries. They will focus the team plan on the most significant family needs that can be met with available resources. The team can also consider the development of additional resources to meet other important concerns in the future.

The Caring Couples Network and the Local Congregation

Caring Couples reach out to others in the name of Jesus Christ. Anything less will destroy the integrity of the Caring Couples Network. The local church is directly involved in the Caring Couples Network Team through its pastor and volunteer couples. Professional consultants may also be members of the church.

The Caring Couples Network Team ministry reaches out to couples at their points of perceived need to provide support, nurture, education, and referrals for resources. The Caring Couples Network Team ministries involve discipleship, pastoral care, evangelism, social concerns, and other aspects of the church's mission.

Having the team closely related to local congregations keeps the basic Christian discipleship focus of the Caring Couples Network. This may be done through the Administrative Council, Council on Ministries, Family Life Committee, or Adult Ministries Council in the local church.

The Caring Couples Network Team is part of the ministry of the local church. The team should be funded through the local church budget. Chapter 14 describes the administrative relationships with the church.

Team Composition: Couples, Pastor, Consultants

The Caring Couples Network Team's effectiveness depends upon the persons who form it. The team consists of three groups who covenant to minister to couples.

1. Pastor and/or other church staff member.
2. Volunteer caring couples.
3. Professional consultants.

The Caring Couples Network Team coordinator may be the pastor or a volunteer couple in the sponsoring church that facilitates details of the team's work. As members of the team, caring couples decide how to coordinate their ministries.

1. Pastor

Pastoral support is essential to the ministry of the Caring Couples Network. The team must have support and involvement from the pastor of the local congregation for several reasons.

The pastor knows:
- The needs of couples, especially those facing transitional stages and crises.
- Potential caring couples and professional consultants who may be available to the Caring Couples Network Team.
- How to link the Caring Couples Network Team with congregation needs.

Clear, positive support from the senior pastor for the Caring Couples Network Team is essential, although another church staff person may facilitate the Caring Couples Network Team ministries.

The Caring Couples Network couples and consultants work in cooperation with the pastor, benefiting from the pastor's guidance and networks. Details of the Caring Couples Network Team operation may be handled by other team members.

The pastor benefits from the Caring Couples Network Team in many ways. Caring Couples, out of their experiences in their own marriages, are in a unique position to provide ministries to couples that greatly expand and supplement the pastor's work with couples. The Caring Couples Network Team benefits from the enabling support and perspectives of the pastor.

2. Caring Couples

Caring Couples are volunteer couples who:
- Commit themselves to grow in their own marriages.
- Want to reach other couples with friendship and support.
- Proclaim the gospel through their personal relationships with others.
- Support Christian spiritual qualities in marriage and family living.
- Seek to improve society's support for healthy marriages and families.

Within each Caring Couple the spouses decide how they function effectively together in reaching other couples. If, because of time availability or personality traits, one spouse is the primary worker in the Caring Couples Network, the other spouse must be wholeheartedly supportive. Both spouses must be involved in Caring Couples Network.

3. Professional Consultants

Professional persons have expertise in such areas as couple therapy, marriage enrichment, family finance, social services, women's shelters, law enforcement, health maintenance, family medicine, and divorce and family mediation. A therapist should be licensed or certified as a psychologist, marriage and family counselor, social worker, pastoral counselor, psychiatrist, or professional counselor.

If the local church does not have any of these professionals among its members, the team may find them in the community or in district or annual conferences.

The professional consultant is available to the Caring Couples Network Team for specialized training and consultation beyond what the pastor and couples already have available among their own resources.

Professional consultants:

- Cooperate with the pastor and couples.
- Provide information about couple dynamics as needed.
- Assist the pastor and couple to connect with community resources.

As much as possible, professionals should be actively involved in a local congregation so the consultants share common faith approaches to Christian marriage with the Caring Couples Network Team. Where this is not possible, the professional consultant should be comfortable in acknowledging and supporting the Christian purposes of the Caring Couples Network Team.

Each team should have access to a professional therapist as a consultant. A team may add other consultants as needed to meet the ministry goals of the Caring Couples Network Team. Professional consultants may train team members, provide backup consultation to Caring Couples, and be available to any Caring Couple for in-depth marital and family assessment and therapy.

Qualifications of Caring Couples Network Team Members

All Caring Couples Network Team members (pastors, couples, consultants) need to:

1. Demonstrate clear commitment to Christian marriage and family values.

2. Be able to incorporate Christian spiritual dimensions of marriage in their work with couples and families.

3. Have experienced in their own marriage the major elements of healthy marriage and family living and be able to identify and nurture these in others.

4. Have understanding and empathy with others.

5. Be committed to the Caring Couples Network concept and support efforts of the Caring Couples Network Team.

Caring Couples Who Participate in the Caring Couples Network Team:

1. Model the qualities of Christian marriage (see Chapter 3).

2. Have been married long enough to give evidence of a healthy relationship with each other and with other family members.

3. Have been active in the local church and willing to volunteer time and resources for friendship and ministry with others.

4. Are able to talk about their Christian faith and understanding of marriage.

5. Are able to share their own experiences in ways that are helpful to others.

6. Are caring and interesting to other couples.

7. Can identify couples and individuals who have significantly nurtured their own growth in marriage.

8. May have special skills or information in finance, health, sexuality, parenting, coping with major dysfunctions, or other areas.

9. May have special insights, resources, and skills from overcoming their own serious marital and/or personal crises, such as alcoholism, abuse, divorce and remarriage, infidelity, illness, financial loss, or career crises.

10. Have been recommended by others who know them well enough to be confident of their ability to serve on the Caring Couples Network Team.

Pastors who sponsor a Caring Couples Network Team:

1. Have a vision of the ways that the Caring Couples Network Team expands ministry with other couples and families. Pastors with this vision will be able to connect caring couples with others who need their friendship and support.

2. Are flexible and comfortable in working with Caring Couples and consultants.

3. Take the initiative in forming a Caring Couples Network Team.

4. Support Caring Couples Network goals and models.

5. Embody the Caring Couple qualities in their own marriages, if married.

6. Are clear about how their spouse will be involved in the Caring Couples Network Team.

7. Use existing discipleship and spiritual nurture programs and organizations in the training and support of Caring Couples.

8. Network with other professionals and agencies in relation to the objectives of the Caring Couples Network Team.

Professional consultants to the Caring Couples Network Team:

1. Contribute competency in specific areas of marriage and family living.

2. Have vision, values, and standards for marriage and family compatible with the Caring Couples Network Team.

3. Are open and comfortable working with volunteer couples, pastors, and churches.

4. Are willing to give volunteer consultation time with the Caring Couples Network Team.

5. Are sensitive to the spiritual and religious dimensions in physical and mental health, finances, and emotional relationships.

6. Network with other professionals and agencies about the objectives of the Caring Couples Network Team.

7. Are well trained in marriage and family assessment, therapy, and enrichment methods and procedures.

Team Organization, Procedures, and Responsibilities

The local Caring Couples Network Team will set its own agenda and priorities for ministry with couples. Each team will meet as often as necessary to structure its ministries and to keep its training current with their ministry goals. (See chapter 5).

The exact distribution of responsibilities and tasks will be made by the local Caring Couples Network Team. In the beginning, the Caring Couples Network Team may need to meet more than once per month. Once in operation, the Caring Couples Network Team may meet as needed to report ministry progress, assess the team ministry plans, and provide mutual encouragement.

The Caring Couple Network Team responsibilities are distributed as follows:

Pastor

1. Organize and sponsor the Caring Couples Network Team.

2. Lead the Caring Couples Network Team to set agenda and priorities for ministries with couples.

3. Facilitate links between Caring Couples Network Team and couples in the parish and community.

4. Include ways to celebrate marriage in the congregation through worship services and special days or programs.

5. Enable networking with other resources and couple needs in the community and in the district/annual conference.

6. Assist the Caring Couples Network Team to arrange specific tasks according to the talents, time, and qualifications of team members.

Caring Couples

1. Pray for and with partner couples.

2. Develop relationships with partner couples.

3. Meet regularly on a friendship basis with each partner couple assigned to them.

4. Invite partner couples to church events; attend with them as appropriate.

5. Obtain training for leadership of specific marriage ministries.

Professional Consultants

1. Provide training and/or consultation to the Caring Couples Network Team.

2. Consult with Caring Couples on their own marriages.

3. Enable networking of Caring Couples Network Team with community resources.

4. Assist couples in referrals.

Focus of Caring Couples Network Teams

Here are some areas and situations that Caring Couples Network Teams can review as they decide where to focus efforts to nurture healthy marriages.

1. Preparation for marriage with adolescents and single adults.

2. Couples considering marriage.

3. Engaged and newlywed couples.

4. Parenting issues for previously married spouses forming step-families.

5. Birth of children and new parent issues.

6. Couples with fertility or pregnancy concerns.

7. Parenting issues with older children, adolescents, young adults.

8. Couples in conflict or considering divorce.

9. Major addictions such as alcoholism and drug abuse.

10. Domestic violence, emotional or sexual abuse, other hurtful patterns.

11. Crises such as death of family member, major accidents or illness.

12. Loss of job, job or career changes, moves to a new location.

13. Empty nest transitions.

14. Couples with aging parents or other intergenerational issues.

15. Retirement and re-engagement options.

16. Marriage and family issues of older adults.

17. Couples with major financial difficulties.

18. Couples with chronic illness or physical challenges.

19. Community disasters and other crises.

20. Other specific couple situations that the Caring Couples Network Team chooses.

The Caring Couples Network Team decides:

- Which outreach ministries to offer in the congregation and community.
- Which issues to address.
- What couples to try to reach.
- How they will do these according to the skills, interests, experiences, and concerns of team members and the needs of the community.

Selecting the Local Caring Couples Network Team Focus

The Caring Couples Network Team may choose to work with any family situation, including those outlined previously. Any of these couples may need the encouragement, models, and friendships that the Caring Couples Network offers. The goal is to assist Partner Couples to succeed in individual, marriage, and family life.

For the start-up phase of a Caring Couples Network Team, it will be best to select specific situations in which to develop ministries. The Caring Couples Network Team should select its focus according to the interests, skills, experiences, and resources of team members in relation to the needs of Partner Couples in the community.

The Caring Couples Network Team seeks to bless and nurture others in every ministry effort. To do this the team needs to consider the following issues as it selects its focus and formulates specific ministry plans:

- Confidentiality. Information and discussion about any couple or situation should be respected and kept confidential.
- Flexibility. The team works to adapt ministry procedures to the levels of skill and interest of both Caring Couples and Partner Couples.

- Cost. Caring Couples are prepared to count the cost of involvement, including money, time, preparation, and commitment.
- Training. The team takes an inventory of additional skills that are needed by Caring Couples and plans training sessions.
- Transfers. The team plans ways to continue ministry contacts when either Partner Couples move or Caring Couples move or are no longer available.

God's Blessings through the Caring Couples Network Team

The heart of the Caring Couples Network is the person-to-person and couple-to-couple relationships among participating couples and families. All resources and plans need to be in the context of the personal ministries which the team members provide.

As Caring Couples Network Teams review the guidelines and suggestions in this handbook, they are encouraged to pray continually for God's blessings through their ministries. Openness to the Holy Spirit's leading in every ministry situation is essential.

Chapter 5
Basic Training for Caring Couples

This chapter will focus on training for the Caring Couples Network Team to equip them to mentor and provide ministries with other couples. Any couple who wants to grow in love is, in a general sense, a Caring Couple.

Basic Tasks for Caring Couples

Caring Couples seek to accomplish five basic tasks in their relationships with Partner Couples. The tasks described here are part of a process of developing a relationship with Partner Couples and encouraging growth in their marriages. The process follows the sequence described here.

Friendship and Rapport with the Couple

Establishing rapport with the Partner Couple initiates the caring process. Both spouses empathize with the other couple, enabling them to feel accepted, respected, and worthwhile. The Caring Couple earns the trust of the Partner Couple by offering them genuine friendship.

Caring Couples must know how to be available to others, to listen well, and to

keep information confidential. Respect, empathy, and positive regard for each person are essential qualities of every Caring Couple.

As friends, the Caring Couple connects with the Partner Couple through common concerns, interests, and experiences. The Caring Couple values and learns from the Partner Couple. A sense of synergy, congruence, affinity, and common concern emerges to form a common bond between couples.

Assessment of the Safety of Family Members

Ministry with the Partner Couple involves determining that every person involved is safe from physical, sexual, and psychological abuse. Domestic violence and sexual abuse are often present but not reported or even recognized. Basic training for Caring Couples includes learning to recognize and respond appropriately to signs of abuse. Consultants and pastors can assist Caring Couples to assess whether any family member is being abused or threatened by abuse. The next steps cannot occur unless abuse is addressed properly.

Abuse includes physical harm or threats of harm, sexual abuse, inappropriate sexual involvements, neglect, and abandonment. When a Caring Couple suspects that these abusive conditions or threats exist, they should confidentially consult with the pastor and/or consultants about appropriate responses to these conditions. Failure to report abuse involves potential criminal liability.

Friendship and rapport assumes that the Caring Couple is safe from physical attack. In most ministry situations, safety for the Caring Couple is assumed. In those occasional situations when danger may be present, the Caring Couple should consult with the pastor and professional consultants.

Renewal of Commitment to Love and Growth

The nurturing process continues as the Caring Couple talks with the Partner Couple about their commitment to grow. This commitment may be their willingness to have friendship contacts with the Caring Couple, to use selected Caring Couples Network resources, to participate in a couples' enrichment group, or to act in ways that will move the couple toward goals of love.

Ideally, the Partner Couple emulates the Caring Couple's commitment to growth in marriage. The Partner Couple can clearly state goals they want as individuals, a couple, and as a family.

Encourage Positive Mutual Affection

Positive mutual affection, respect, and support are essential for success in marriage and family living. Caring Couples demonstrate positive affection in many

ways, including smiles, politeness, kind words, and warm touching. Other couples may also do this well, yet when difficulties arise may forget to express affection.

Love is most essential when it is least available. Caring Couples can note the positive expressions that do occur and encourage the couple to increase them. This forms a hopeful context in which conflicts and difficulties can be addressed.

Help Connect Couples to Vital Resources

Caring Couples are friends who know enough about resources the Partner Couple needs to make referrals for help. Caring Couples link other couples to available information, agencies, and other assistance. Knowing the resources described in this handbook plus those of the community gives the Caring Couple confidence in ministering to Partner Couples.

Approaches to Preparation

Since each Caring Couples Network Team has the freedom and responsibility to establish its own goals, the specific approaches to training team members will vary. The common goal is to have competent Caring Couples who minister well to a variety of needs. There are usually several good approaches for achieving this competency goal.

Instead of a specific method of training, the Caring Couples Network emphasizes basic and advanced relationship skills. By describing desired competencies, Caring Couples Network Team participants can select married couples who have these qualities and suggest ways for them to increase their skills.

Basic Caring Couples Network Training

Initial basic competencies for Caring Couples are:

1. Accurate self-knowledge (as individuals and as a couple).

2. A basic understanding of the Caring Couples Network.

Basic Goal 1: Accurate Self-Knowledge

Method: A Caring Couple can grow in understanding themselves and their marriage by using the resources listed in Chapters 6–9. A Caring Couples Network Team may participate in the communication exercises as a group.

Caring Couples should be trained to take an inventory of their own marriages to grow in being open, candid, and honest with each other. In exploring their marriage relationship, couples respond to the following questions:

- What do we do well? Not so well?
- How do we use our own marriage experiences to grow in love?
- How can we assist others to grow in love?
- Where do we want to improve now?
- What do we celebrate as our strengths, values, and accomplishments?
- How do these illustrate God's presence in our marriage and family?

After carefully considering their own marriage, a Caring Couple may invite feedback from other Caring Couples Network Team members.

Caring Couples must know how to be available to others, to listen well, and to keep information confidential. Respect, empathy, and positive regard for each person are essential basic qualities of Caring Couples. These qualities are nurtured through a thorough self-knowledge.

The training requires Caring Couples to go through the same nurture process that they will later share with other couples. This Caring Couples Network process enables couples to consider their own strengths and growth needs in private without having to discuss their own marriage situation with others. A couple may decide to seek help for themselves if needed.

If married, the pastor and spouse should also participate in these training opportunities. If not married, the pastor should participate in equivalent growth experiences in relation to couples' ministries.

Basic Goal 2: A Basic Understanding of the Caring Couples Network

Method. A Caring Couples Network orientation program enables Caring Couples to know the range of marriage ministries envisioned for the team.

These basics may be learned in a one-day retreat or study setting using the *Caring Couples Network Videotape,* this *Caring Couples Network Handbook,* and locally developed statements of goals.

Continuing Caring Couples Network Training

The three goals of ongoing Caring Couples Network training are:

1. Continued personal and couple growth.

2. Specialized training for mentoring specific types of couples.

3. Supervision and feedback concerning work with other couples.

Continuing training procedures assume that Caring Couples will be "mentor couples." Caring Couples will relate to specific types of couples, such as premarital/newlywed couples, parents, or couples in crisis.

Continuing Goal 1: Continuing Personal and Couple Growth

Methods. Caring Couples will continue to grow by examining their own marriage and using Caring Couples Network resources, marriage inventories, communication skills training, spiritual growth retreats, and other experiential study programs that nurture a couple's marital and spiritual growth. Caring Couples should participate in some type of marriage enrichment or couple growth experience, couples class, marriage seminar, or marital therapy.

Participation (at least every year or two) in a "Celebrating Marriage," "Marriage Encounter," or other marriage enrichment event is valuable to a couple at any stage of marriage. Attendance at an "Engaged Encounter" weekend may help the caring couple understand newlywed issues.

Continuing Goal 2: Specialized Training for Mentoring Specific Types of Couples

Methods. Additional preparation as appropriate to the couple's interests, skills, and goals for ministry with other couples may be in one or more of these areas:

- Training and supervision in leading a couple's communication class.
- Supervised training in giving feedback on marital inventories.

- Preparation for teaching specific topics for couples, such as finances, sexuality, parenting, and career and marriage.
- Training in working with couples in abusive and other troubling situations, under the supervision of appropriate professionals.
- Specialized study in pastoral care programs such as lay counseling training and professional skills continuing education.

In consultation with the Caring Couples Network Team, each Caring Couple decides how much additional training it needs in order to be prepared to minister with selected couple situations that may be the focus of the Caring Couples Network Team ministry. This specialized training should be arranged according to the couple's mentoring interests, specific goals, and available resources.

Continuing Goal 3: Supervision and Feedback Concerning Work with Partner Couples

Methods: Regular meetings of the Caring Couples Network Team need to allow time for Caring Couples to process their own feelings and experiences in working with Partner Couples. These feedback and supervision times must be confidential and limited to the Caring Couples Network Team members so Caring Couples can receive specific suggestions about their work.

The professional consultants to the Caring Couples Network Team should help establish guidelines and provide supervision for the activities of the team.

Much valuable feedback may be obtained from role-playing. Participants may offer observations about process, responses, emotional reactions, and other aspects of the situation. This is even more useful when the role play is videotaped and available for playback as part of the discussion. Caring Couples learn much from discussing videotapes of couple interaction in counseling settings, movies, and other media.

Each team can adapt these continuing education and training possibilities to its own Caring Couples Network Team. In addition, joint meetings of several Caring Couples Network Teams may be arranged to accomplish some of these training possibilities.

Chapter 6
Using the Caring Couples Network Video

The Caring Couples Network Video introduces the network to interested persons. The video is intended to inform, inspire, and invite. It is available through Discipleship Resources. *The Caring Couples Network Video* will:

- **Inform.** The video describes Caring Couples and their characteristics.
- **Inspire.** The video gives a positive view of marriage. Marriage is a God-given transformational relationship in which we continue to learn to love spouse as neighbor in the context of God's grace and love to us.
- **Invite.** The video offers the viewer specific ways to participate in the Caring Couples Network.

The Caring Couples Network Video is about fifteen minutes long. The video discusses the marriage crisis, describes the qualities of Caring Couples, and invites participation in the Caring Couples Network. The viewing guide that comes with the *Caring Couples Network Video* provides additional details and suggestions for using the video.

Part I: Marriage: For Better or Worse?

On their wedding day few couples plan to break up. Yet of some 2.3 million couples who marry each year, more than half will fail through divorce or separation (McManus, *Marriage Savers,* 30).

Each couple has choices about daily life, big and little events, and the direction of their lifelong marriage journey.

Questions for Discussion

1. Remember special memories about your dating, wedding, and early marriage years, or about couples you know.

2. Of the couples you know well, how many (percentage) are:
   - Succeeding and really happy?
   - So-so, neither happy nor divorced?
   - Divorced or very unhappy?

3. Think of some couples who are succeeding in their marriages. What factors contribute to their success? What is your church doing to support these healthy marriages?

4. Think of other couples who have divorced, are having major difficulties, or seem unhappy most of the time. What factors contribute to these negative outcomes? What is your church doing to minister to these unhealthy marriages?

5. What are some effects of divorce on children, society, all of us?

Part II: Qualities of Caring Couples

From Chapter 3 we learn that caring couples are growing, communicating, negotiating, renewing, learning, and reaching out.

Questions for Discussion

1. What are other descriptions for caring, loving couples?

2. In what ways is marriage a "work in progress"? . . . a "life journey"? . . . a "dance"? . . . other marriage metaphors?

3. In which areas are you doing well? Which would you especially want to change or improve?

1. Growing in Love

As Caring Couples we want to grow in love with God, each other, our families, and our neighbors. Every couple wants to succeed in marriage. Few want to fail, quit, divorce, or hurt each other, but they do not know how to succeed. Many do not know how to give as well as receive.

Questions for Discussion

1. What are your desires and goals for your own marriage? Which have you achieved?

2. What are some desires and goals of couples you know?

3. How could you help them reach goals in ways that encourage them?

2. Communicating

As Caring Couples, we learn how to communicate honestly in love. We learn that negative "you" messages hurt partners and put them down, sometimes driving them away. We also learn that positive "I" messages affirm and support partners, drawing them closer. We learn that both the message and way it's delivered are equally important.

Questions for Discussion

1. Have you ever seen spouses hurt each other?

2. What are some "put-downs" you have seen? (Negatives: forgetting things, interrupting someone viewing TV, watching TV instead of talking with one's partner, ignoring, yelling, hitting, threatening to hit, and calling someone names.)

3. When have you seen spouses communicate care and love? (Positive: "I" messages express clearly what one needs or thinks. They uphold the partner and express that he or she is as important as the speaker. Examples include the following: "Would you like . . . ?" "Thank you!" "Please." Positive communication may involve speaking softly, asking if another person has time to visit, hugs, choices rather than demands, and offers to compromise.

3. Negotiating Goals and Problem Solving

As Caring Couples, we learn to negotiate mutually beneficial goals and resolve conflicts. It is not a question of whether conflicts and problems will come. They do come. It is essential to be able to cope with conflicts in ways that are reconciling. We seek to imitate God's grace. Just as God continues to forgive us, reconcile us, and bring us together again, we seek to be reconciled with each other.

Questions for Discussion

1. Some have said that there are no conflicts or problems, only differences in values and priorities. What do you think?

2. Do you feel *demands* on you? Do you *defer* to your *"demander"*? Does your partner *demand* that you do things his or her way? Can you talk together easily? When do you want to hide or get away? Does one partner minimize issues or blow things way out of proportion?

3. What are some of the forces that pull partners apart?

4. Renewing Our Commitment

As Caring Couples, we seek to deepen our commitment to our marriage covenant and to nurture each other through our life journeys. In the wedding vows couples promise to stay together. They pledge to create a safe, dependable place for love to grow. The Christian faith invites couples to love each other as God has loved us.

Questions for Discussion

1. Which of these outcomes fits most of the couples you know?
   - **Negative:** "If things keep going like they are, we'll be broken up by then, as all our friends have."
   - **Positive:** "Regardless of what happens, we know we will be together both now and later."

2. What helps spouses to renew and deepen their commitment to each other? What are some of the things that gradually push partners apart?

3. How could couples discover whether their long-term goals fit together?

5. Learning and Nurturing

As Caring Couples, we use the Bible, spiritual disciplines, and other resources and events to nurture our marriages toward these goals. Among the resources for growth are Bible study, prayer, reading, church activities, spending time together (and apart), and visiting with friends and relatives. Chapters 7–9 offer additional growth resources.

Questions for Discussion

1. What resources for growth are you presently using?

2. What Bible references point to caring couple qualities? (Examples include 1 Corinthians 7 and 13, Romans 12, Ephesians 5, and 1 John 4.)

3. What are some activities your church has to help couples? What program or activities could be done as couples as well as individuals?

6. Reaching Out to Others

As Caring Couples, we mutually support others in helping fellow couples and families. Caring Couples seek to be agents of peace, justice, equality, empowerment, faithfulness, and freedom for individuals, couples, and families.

Questions for Discussion

1. When have you assisted others to get help for a certain problem?

2. What help would you most like to receive for your marriage?

3. When have you felt all alone? Who helped to brighten your life? Do you know couples who seem to be lonely? How can you reach out to them?

Part III: Invite: Sharing Caring Couples Network Ministries

Questions for Discussion

1. Would you like to learn better ways to care for your own marriage? What specific help do you need for your marriage?

2. What resources do you already use in your marriage?

3. What is your congregation doing to strengthen marriages?

Chapter 7
Basic Caring Couples Network Resources

Resources of Caring Couples Network Team Ministries

Caring Couples Network Handbook. This volume offers details of Caring Couples Network Team organization and ministries.

Caring Couples Network Video. The video describes qualities of caring couples and introduces the Caring Couples Network.

"Caring Couples Network" brochure. This flier briefly outlines the Caring Couples Network and the steps to get started.

Resources for Couples to Grow

"Celebrating Marriage," "Marriage Encounter: United Methodist," and "Engaged Encounter: United Methodist." Chapter 8 outlines these weekend marriage enrichment experiences.

Growing Love in Christian Marriage. This book and computer disk are designed for any couple (both marital and pre-marital) to use to grow and explore issues in their relationship. The *Growing Love in Christian Marriage* interactive computer disk supplements the printed text. This disk contains the following information:

- Basic marriage inventory questions with immediate scoring for scales.
- Interactive versions of selected EXPLORE exercises in the text.
- The couple's introductory questionnaire.
- A guide to Bible reading for couples.
- Prayers and other home worship resources for couples.
- References to books and periodicals.
- General viewers' guide for movies and drama.

Chapter 8
Caring Couples Network and Marriage Enrichment

Marriage enrichment refers to any type of activity that assists couples to grow in love and care for each other, their families, and others they meet. The Caring Couples Network is directly related to two types of marriage enrichment programs, "Celebrating Marriage" and "Marriage Encounter: United Methodist." Additional resources are described in Chapter 9.

Celebrating Marriage

The "Celebrating Marriage" program provides small group and couple sharing in a marriage enrichment event. Since 1982 "Celebrating Marriage" has been a marriage enrichment weekend program of the General Board of Discipleship. During this time over a hundred leader couples have been certified, and thousands of couples have participated in events. It provides a solid basis for several flexible formats that expand its availability across the church.

One goal of every Caring Couples Network Team is to sponsor or co-sponsor at least one "Celebrating Marriage" event every year. Participating in a marriage enrichment event annually will refresh and renew caring couples as well as demonstrate to other couples the value of these opportunities for growth.

Couples always lead "Celebrating Marriage." Formerly, certification of leaders was guided and recorded at the national level. In 1996 this was changed to place full responsibility for leader quality on the local Caring Couples Network Team, or clusters of Caring Couples Network Teams.

The *Celebrating Marriage Manual* provides details of the leader qualifications and complete guidelines for conducting a "Celebrating Marriage" event in any of the formats described below.

Caring Couples who lead a "Celebrating Marriage" event should meet these qualifications and guidelines:

1. Be active members of a Caring Couples Network Team.

2. Have previously been a participant couple in a "Celebrating Marriage" or equivalent marriage enrichment event.

3. In preparing to lead a "Celebrating Marriage" event, receive consultation and guidance from an experienced "Celebrating Marriage" leader couple.

4. For the new leader couple's first "Celebrating Marriage" event, have other Caring Couples Network Team couples attend and provide constructive feedback.

5. For each event the leader couple should be open to feedback from participants and have an evaluation questionnaire

or other method for obtaining suggestions for improving the events they lead.

There are several possible "Celebrating Marriage" event formats:

- Friday evening through Sunday noon.
- Friday evening through Saturday afternoon or evening.
- Saturday morning through Sunday afternoon.
- All day Saturday (morning through afternoon or evening).
- A series of evening sessions, usually one session per week.

Overnight formats allow more concentrated time for couples with fewer potential interruptions, yet are usually more difficult for couples to attend. Those who are willing to give the additional effort and expense for a weekend event usually find it worthwhile.

One-day formats may enable additional couples to participate although there is less time available.

A **series of weekly sessions** gives participating couples much more opportunity to practice what they learn in the sessions and obtain support and feedback about these real-life applications. Since sessions are mixed in with the rest of weekly living, some couples may miss sessions or not have time to concentrate when they do attend.

Any of these formats may be conducted at a retreat, hotel, or church location. The benefits of a relaxing retreat location must be weighed against the additional expense of overnight accommodations.

A local church location avoids overnight expenses, but it may be considered too disruptive since participants would return home each evening.

A hotel location may have better overnight accommodations but be more expensive than a retreat location. Some hotel locations may also have recreational features usually found at retreat settings.

Celebrating Marriage for Newlywed Couples

The "Celebrating Marriage" event for newlywed couples might be distinguished from other "Celebrating Marriage" events. This event for recently married couples may utilize the "Celebrating Marriage" resources as well as adapt topics from the *Growing Love in Christian Marriage* book and computer disk.

Celebrating Marriage for Step-Family Couples

A "Celebrating Marriage" event planned primarily for second-marriage and step-family couples allows them to consider issues unique to second-marriage couples.

Celebrating Marriage for Later-Life Marriages

"Celebrating Marriage" events for later-life marriages addresses issues for maturing couples and may have more flexibility in scheduling.

To order "Celebrating Marriage" materials, contact the Discipleship Resources Distribution Center.

Marriage Encounter and Engaged Encounter

"Marriage Encounter: United Methodist" (MEUM) is the United Methodist expression of Marriage Encounter. The event is led by couples trained in this program. MEUM was established in 1976 and has been an affiliate of the General Board of Discipleship since 1978. The weekend program, led by two or three lay couples and a United Methodist clergy and spouse, extends from Friday evening until late afternoon Sunday. Events are usually held in a motel or retreat center, allowing privacy for each couple.

Presenting couples share methods and opportunities for deep private communication between the husband and wife, making it easier to find trust, confidence, and understanding. This weekend away from the usual everyday pressures and interruptions helps deepen, renew, and revitalize the couple relationship.

A "Deepening Our Vision of Encounter" (DOVE) weekend is for couples who have previously attended MEUM and want to experience continued growth in their marriage.

"Engaged Encounter: United Methodist" (EEUM), a program of MEUM, is available for engaged couples, those thinking of marriage, and those married less than two years. The EEUM weekend begins on Friday evening and ends late Sunday afternoon. The location may be a church, retreat center, or motel that allows the two partners to focus on each other as a couple and look at marriage as a covenant. The EEUM was started in 1984 in Tucson, Arizona.

These weekends provide presentations by the leaders, private times for each individual to write responses to questions concerning personal and marriage growth, and separate time for each couple to discuss these. Telephone: (800) 795–LOVE.

Essential Qualities of Marriage Enrichment Events

Setting
- A location conducive to openness, relaxation, renewal.
- Child care as needed to relieve couples from concern about their children.
- Good food (prepared, catered, pot luck, etc.).
- If overnight, prefer private sleeping rooms for couples.
- Reasonable cost.
- Convenient travel.

Leader Qualities
- Couples who model good marriages.
- Good content that stimulates couples to consider issues.
- Resources, materials, handouts that enable couples to remember content.
- Leaders trained and experienced in the type of event they lead.

Schedule and Format
- Group time as couples, same-sex groups, and mixed groups to share perspectives.
- Worship times to draw couples closer to God.
- Fun time (singing, games, etc.) for group-spirit building.
- Free time for individual couples to talk, consider issues.

The leadership team for the event may use content modules and exercise units from many sources to plan the event. Leadership for this event should be Caring Couples Network couples who have previously attended a "Celebrating Marriage" or equivalent event and who consult with experienced leaders in planning and conducting the "Celebrating Marriage" event.

Special Topics

In addition to the marriage enrichment events previously described, the following special topic events could be developed in celebration of marriage and family:

- Parenting concerns and issues focusing on children, adolescents, blended families, specifically challanged children, children with chronic illnesses, adolescents with behaviorial problems, and gifted children.
- Marriage and "three generation households."
- Remarriage and step-parenting issues.
- Empty-nest marriage and other transitional stages.
- Marriage and finances, dual career, career changes.
- Marriage and recovery from alcoholism, extra-marital sexual affairs, or mental illness.
- Marriage in retirement years; illness and death of spouse.
- Singles considering marriage.

Chapter 9 provides information about other marriage enrichment programs and resources.

The Caring Couples Network intends to provide a wide variety of approaches for couples' ministries. Couples and families need so much nurture and support that the Caring Couples Network wants to make our circle larger and cooperate to bring marriage and family ministries to all. Churches are encouraged to offer programs for marriage preparation and for nourishing existing marriages.

People often fear being displaced or excluded more than change itself. When couples are nurtured and taught, they learn new patterns for making their marriages strong and healthy, which encourages them to share their successes with others.

Marriage Enrichment

In addition to the United Methodist "Celebrating Marriage" program, "Marriage Encounter: United Methodist" and "Engaged Encounter: United Methodist," several ecumenical resources for marriage enrichment leadership are listed here.

A.C.M.E. (Association for Couples in Marriage Enrichment).

The Association for Couples in Marriage Enrichment (A.C.M.E.) is a resource for training marriage enrichment leaders, providing resource materials, and encouraging healthy marriages. Building healthy, enduring marital relationships is the purpose of A.C.M.E. David and Vera Mace, founders of A.C.M.E., emphasize that "through better marriages come better families, and through better families comes a stronger, healthier society in which to live" (*Toward Better Marriages,* 32).

The A.C.M.E. certification process ensures that leader couples have participated in A.C.M.E. events and have prepared and co-led at least one marriage enrichment weekend under the supervision of a certified leader couple. There are many A.C.M.E.-certified leader couples across the U.S.

Caring Couples will benefit from becoming members of A.C.M.E. and receiving the *A.C.M.E. Newsletter* and information about marriage resources, workshops, and leader-training events. A.C.M.E. has many local and regional groups. Trained leader couples may be consultants to Caring Couples

Network Teams and may be available to lead marriage enrichment events.

More information about membership, resources, newsletter, and leader couples is available from the Association for Couples in Marriage Enrichment, 502 North Broad St., P.O. Box 10596, Winston-Salem, NC 27108. Telephone: (910) 724–1526 and (800) 634–8325.

Recovery of Hope

The Recovery of Hope program offers a Saturday morning program for couples whose marriages are seriously troubled and on the verge of divorce. The half-day program usually has three presenter couples who describe some of the major troubles they faced and how they are overcoming them to make their marriages more satisfying and healthy. Professional therapists consult with couples about the next steps in healing their own marriages.

Some Recovery of Hope centers also offer intensive week-long programs for distressed couples.

Information about Recovery of Hope programs may be obtained from the Recovery of Hope network office, 283 S. Butler Rd., P.O. Box 550, Mount Gretna, PA 17064. Telephone: (800) 327–2590.

Marriage Savers

Concepts of mentor couples helping other couples are presented and publicized by Michael McManus through the Marriage Savers program. A Caring Couples Network Team will benefit from knowing about the cooperative efforts this program emphasizes.

Caring Couples are "marriage savers" in many ways. The Caring Couples Network Team is designed to address many of the marriage and family needs that are described by McManus. An informative book and video series may be obtained from Marriage Savers Institute, 9500 Michael's Court, Bethesda, MD 20817. Telephone: (301) 469–5870.

Selected Books

For more extensive bibliographies of books dealing with marriage topics, see the following:

Dunn, Dick and Betty. *Willing to Try Again: Steps toward Blending a Family.* Valley Forge, Pa.: Judson Press, 1994. Considers the many dimensions of step-families and ways the couple and their children adjust to their new family situation.

Everett, William J. *Blessed be the Bond: Christian Perspectives on Marriage and Family.* Lanham, Md.: University Press of America, 1990. A theology of marriage as sacrament, vocation, covenant, and communion.

Hendrix, Harville. *Getting the Love You Want.* New York: Harper, 1988. Describes the "Imago" approach to marriage which sees marriage as a way to complete the unfinished work of childhood, grow toward maturity, and transform one's relationship into a fully conscious marriage using personal and spiritual resources. Many exercises are included.

Hendrix, Harville. *Keeping the Love You Find,* 1992. An application of the "Imago" relationship principles to single and divorced persons who seek a better marriage. Many practical exercises are provided.

Hunt, Richard and Joan. *Awaken Your Power to Love,* 1994. How faith and values are keys to marriage is explored in five dimensions of marriage: Choosing your future, evaluating your resources, increasing positives, eliminating negatives, and connecting through communication. Many exercises and questions for discussion from this book are included on the *Growing Love in Christian Marriage* computer disk.

Lederach, Naomi and John. *Recovery of Hope,* 1991. A collection of stories about fifteen couples across North America who have participated in the Recovery of Hope program. Available from Good Books, P.O. Box 419, Intercourse, PA 17534–0419. Telephone: (800) 762–7171.

Markman, Howard, Scott Stanley, and Susan Blumberg. *Fighting for Your Marriage.* San Francisco: Jossey-Bass, 1994. Based on long-term research about the PREP ("Prevention and Relationship Enhancement Program") marriage communication and commitment workshops, this book describes positive steps for preventing divorce and preserving a lasting marriage. Clear guidelines, helpful questions, and exercises are included.

McManus, Michael J. *Marriage Savers.* Revised Edition. Grand Rapids: Zondervan, 1995. A fact-packed book that challenges churches to take specific steps to strengthen marriages as the foundation for strong families. It lists many effective marriage-saving programs.

Wilke, Steve and Dave and Neta Jackson. *Recovering Hope in Your Marriage.* New Leaf Press, 1993. A Recovery of Hope series of booklets containing true stories about couples who saved their marriages. Topics include alcohol abuse, communication, fighting, trust, and new vision.

Marriage Magazines and Newsletters

The following magazines contain stories about how couples cope with specific issues, information about marriage encounter events, and related resources for couples and others who seek to minister with couples and families:

Marriage is published monthly by International Marriage Encounter, Inc., 955 Lake Drive, Saint Paul, MN 55120.

Marriage Partnership is published by *Christianity Today,* Inc., 465 Gundersen Drive, Carol Stream, IL 60188. Telephone (708) 260–0114.

The *A.C.M.E. Newsletter* is available as part of membership in the Association for Couples in Marriage Enrichment, 502 North Broad St., P.O. Box 10596, Winston-Salem, NC 27108. Telephone: (800) 634–8325.

Chapter 10
A Program for Engaged and Newlywed Couples—First Married and Previously Married

Pre-Wedding and Early Marriage: Two Phases in One Process

The newlywed focus needs to begin with the initial pre-wedding contact with a couple and extend through the first two years of marriage. This two-year period is a major opportunity for the Caring Couples Network Team to support couples as they start their marriage journey. At least one Caring Couple should be in continuous friendship with each newlywed couple, beginning as soon as possible before their wedding.

The first two years of marriage are especially important because spouses make important changes as they grow together as a couple. The importance of succeeding in these years is emphasized by the fact that nearly half of all divorces occur during these first two years of marriage.

Both pre-wedding and post-wedding support ministries are important and should not be separated. In the context of the couple's development during these initial twenty-four to thirty months, the wedding can be seen as being part of this sequence. Planning a two-year-plus process removes the pressure to do everything prior to the wedding, often without any follow-up after the wedding.

The following resources can be used according to the couple's situation and in accordance with the policies concerning weddings and marriage that your local team and community sets.

The Caring Couples Network Team as a Channel for God's Blessings

In the service of Christian marriage, the pastor invites the congregation of relatives and friends to support and nurture the married couple throughout their lives. The Caring Couples Network's purpose is to share this blessing with couples at every stage of their marital journey and family development. God blesses couples who care and share their experience, support, and friendship with other couples.

The Caring Couples Network assumes that all participating couples want to grow in their marriages. Each couple can learn from other couples, regardless of age or experience. In this sense, newlywed couples are growing to become Caring Couples.

The couples who join the local Caring Couples Network Team have experience in marriage and training in specific skills for assisting other couples. With the pastor these Caring Couples provide structured leadership for ministry with engaged and newlywed couples.

Caring Couples Ministry with Newlywed Couples

Any local church with engaged couples can develop a ministry for them. Since group activities are a desirable part of the two-year-plus program, churches may cooperate to provide these during the year as needed.

The program outlined here assumes that the pastor leads in facilitating these contacts between Caring Couples and engaged or newlywed couples. These materials may be used by the pastor and engaged couple or with the help of the Caring Couple.

A Cooperative Team Ministry: Pastor and Caring Couples

The ministry with engaged and newly-wed couples is a cooperative team ministry of the pastor and the caring couples. Together they decide which components of ministry with engaged and newlywed couples are best provided by the pastor and which by the Caring Couples. Based on the number of engaged and newlywed couples a church has in any twelve-month period, the pastor and the team can plan events for individual couples and for groups of couples.

The pastor's initial contact with an engaged couple gives an opportunity to introduce the couple to the Caring Couples Network approach and its program for supporting couples. The pastor can provide the couple a copy of *Growing Love in Christian Marriage*, along with information about the local premarital/newlywed couple nurturing programs and the wedding policies of the church.

The pastor can describe to the engaged or newlywed couple which Caring Couples are available to relate to them and the procedure for introducing them. The initial meeting between Caring Couple and engaged or newlywed Partner Couple may be set up by either the pastor or Caring Couple, according to the plan of the pastor and team. If several Caring Couples are available, the engaged or newlywed couple may select the couple that seems best for them.

In the Caring Couple's initial contact with the engaged or newlywed couple, details of schedule and use of *Growing Love in Christian Marriage* and other resources can be arranged. In this get-acquainted session, both couples can share experiences and perspectives informally in the sponsor couple's home, at church, over a dinner, or in another informal setting.

The premarital couple may be invited to consider many ways of viewing marriage (such as covenant, journey, commitment) and the role of communication in connecting their future (goals), and their resources (skills, personality, families of origin, etc.) for increasing positives and decreasing negatives.

The sponsoring Caring Couple could share their views on the meanings of the marriage service (wedding) and exchange examples of how they have experienced the covenant and commitment aspects of marriage. The Caring Couple can describe how they would like to support the couple and invite suggestions from the couple.

Following the initial get-aquainted meeting, sessions can be held conjointly with the individual couple and the Caring Couple or designed as group sessions for several couples. The Caring Couples Network Team and pastor schedule primary leadership for subsequent sessions.

The leadership of these group sessions will probably come from Caring Couples, pastors, consultants, and other resource persons. In each session there should be opportunity for leader couples to describe experiences they have had that are relevant to the topics, as well as group sharing of viewpoints and experiences.

These sessions may be designed for both engaged and newlywed couples. Scheduling of group sessions needs to be done in relation to the number of participating couples, since weddings occur throughout the year. Several churches may work together to arrange group sessions, according to the number of engaged couples who are ready for them.

Using Growing Love in Christian Marriage

Topics in Growing Love in Christian Marriage can be considered in five to ten group or individual couple sessions. The following outline provides for ten sessions matched to the chapters in Growing Love in Christian Marriage. Additional sessions may be needed to consider issues of step-families and second marriages.

The session numbers and chapter references are the same as listed in Growing Love in Christian Marriage. It is essential to encourage couples to use "Explore" and other practice activities selected from the Growing Love in Christian Marriage couple's book and computer disk between sessions.

The pastor and Caring Couples can adapt the outline to fit the needs of their Partner Couples. Topics can be presented in evening, half-day or full-day sessions,

weekend events, church-night series, or a couples' class. The structure and schedule will also depend upon how paired couples will use couple-to-couple meetings.

Group Session 1: Marriage as Lifetime Journey (Chapters 1 and 11)

A brief review of the Caring Couples Network Team approach as it is structured in the local situation can begin this session. The Caring Couples Network Video can be useful to elicit views of marriage.

The primary focus of the session is on the meanings of marriage and how these relate to the wedding service and other visions of Christian marriage. The foundational role of commitment to God and each other concerning the covenant of marriage can be presented.

Group Session 2: What Do We Bring to Our Marriage?

The two major sets of resources that persons bring to marriage are (1) personal qualities, habits, and skills and (2) family of origin (and previous marriage, if any), relationships and dynamics.

Checklists in the Growing Love in Christian Marriage book and disk may be used to help persons become more aware of how each impacts her or his partner. Skits illustrating typical problem areas, surprises, or other personality issues may open discussion about interpersonal issues in humorous ways.

Family-of-origin influences on marriage may be introduced by having each person prepare a genogram or family tree of at least their own, their parents', and their grandparents' generations. This overview may help couples see any recurring events among family members (accomplishments, education, job changes, divorces, etc.), talk about family relationships, and how these patterns may influence the ways the new couple might interact with each other, relatives, and in-laws.

Group Session 3:
What Are Our Expectations?

Comparing expectations, assumptions, and goals helps a couple find common values and anticipate potential conflicts. This session links family of origin and personal habits to expectations and standards for marriage success or failure that each couple has. The session may also allow participants to consider how goals and expectations for marriage can be modified across the lifetime marriage journey and how they are related to a couple's background, friends, work, and other dimensions of living.

Leader couples can describe some of their own assumptions about marriage and how they have identified and used their common goals in constructive ways as well as how they cope with conflicts between their goals.

Group Session 4:
How Do We Communicate?

Basic couple communication skills can be considered in this session. Among these are speaker-listener skills, awareness of one's impact on her or his partner, attention to private meanings and "code words" between spouses, and other aspects of communication.

Group Session 5:
All Couples Change, and It's Tough!

Problem-solving and conflict-resolution skills can be illustrated with skits by leader couples and by illustrations or film excerpts from current or recent movies. Providing couples opportunity to practice negotiating an actual change along with feedback to them from leaders and/or other couples should be part of this session.

Group Session 6:
Uncovering Our Sexuality

This session considers how affectionate needs, intimacy, personal space, and sexual appetites and desires are related to marriage quality. The many ways in which affection and affirmation are expressed in the couple's sexual and other activities can be presented by leader couples. Sexuality as God's gift to couples for support and nourishment can be emphasized. Current information about sexual functioning, sexually transmitted diseases, and other sexual matters may be presented by professional consultants with opportunity for questions and discussion.

Group Session 7:
Money, Possessions, and Work

Finances and career issues are central to marriage, and they need to be presented from a Christian stewardship perspective. Leader couples may describe how their values are expressed in their careers, their money management, and decisions about tithing and stewardship in relation to the church and the world's needs. This session may also consider the ways in which work schedules and demands affect marriage quality. A family financial consultant may be a resource leader for this session.

Group Session 8:
Children and Others

The complex relationships between marriage and parenting apply to all couples whether they have (or plan to have) their own children. According to the needs of participants, step-family issues may be part of this session or may be considered in additional sessions for couples where one or both partners already have children.

Group Session 9:
Here Comes Everyone!

Friendship networks are very important to couples. The church is one of the major networks of support as couples form friendships with other couples. How the couple arranges leisure time, celebrations, family contacts, and other elements of their marriage can be addressed by leader couples and discussion. Classes and other events for couples can be announced or organized.

Group Session 10:
Sneak Preview of the Years Ahead

Marriage as a lifelong journey for growing in love can bring all of these topics together as couples anticipate changes at each stage of life. Although couples may be preoccupied with current matters, a long-term view allows an opportunity to place the many elements of marriage into patterns and relationships that nourish growth and increase loving contributions to each other, family, friends, community, and the world in the context of their Christian commitment.

Training Caring Couples for Ministry with Premarital and Newlywed Couples

Caring couples who sponsor another couple need appropriate training. This training is based on the qualities the Caring Couples bring to the program. Caring Couples Network Team training includes the experiences provided through the *Growing Love in Christian Marriage* sessions outlined previously.

Caring Couples may provide leadership on specific topics, including communication skills, spiritual formation, family relations, sexuality, or marriage inventory feedback. The Caring Couples Network Team can take an inventory of the leadership skills among the Caring Couples and plan ways to combine these skills to provide leadership for events offered to partner couples. Additional training provided by consultants and workshops is required. The Caring Couples Network Team allows flexibility in using available resources and in obtaining necessary training to accomplish the ministries for Partner Couples.

One guideline for training is that a Caring Couple should first experience the type of activity they plan to lead. This enables the Caring Couple to be aware of issues in its own marriage and sensitive to the feelings of Partner Couples. Training can be provided by the Caring Couples Network Team, consultants, or workshops.

Previously Married Couples and Step-Families

In addition to the issues that all couples face, persons who have been married before and/or who have children must consider additional issues. Some of these issues are:

- What current role does the ex-mate now play in the current marriage?
- If one spouse has children but the other does not, how are the roles and responsibilities negotiated?
- If both spouses have their own children, what roles and responsibilities must be negotiated?

In creating ministries to premarital and early-marriage couples, a Caring Couples Network Team can provide variations that may be needed by couples who are forming step-families.

Caring Couples Network Team Policies

It should be clear that the church expects all couples to be involved in the engaged/newlywed program. This policy gives clear encouragement to the premarital couple to participate in the Caring Couples Network ministries. A premarital or newlywed couple that refuses to participate in any aspect of the program may be signaling that it is not ready for marriage.

Each program can identify the elements that are essential for all premarital couples who are married in the church or by its pastor and the point at which first ministry with them begins. When a church and/or community adopts a "community marriage policy" (see Chapter 19), the importance of the premarital/newlywed ministry program is emphasized.

The Caring Couples Network Team can provide printed information about:
- The elements of the program for nurturing all engaged and newlywed couples.
- Information about additional supports for couples where one or both partners were previously married,

living together, and/or already have children.
- Policies for the payment for use of the church, musicians, custodians, and other items involved in the wedding itself.
- How their ministries work with the premarital and newlywed pastoral counseling and care provided by the pastoral staff.
- How the team relates to the church wedding consultant, if any.

Newlywed Couples' Post-wedding Years One and Two

During the first two years after the wedding, continuing friendship contacts (at least every three months) with the sponsor Caring Couple help the newlywed couple to connect to additional resources according to their needs. The Caring Couple can invite the newlywed couple to dinner, recreational events, or other activities as support for the couple.

Continuing Friendship and Support

The major purpose in these follow-up contacts is to enable the newlywed couple to function increasingly as a couple and form support networks with other couples. Each newlywed couple's need for Caring Couples Network Team support will vary according to the desires and skills of the couple, the proximity of relatives and other couple friends, and the work, education, and other commitments of the newlywed couple.

The other major purpose is to assure the newlywed couple that they can consult as needed with their sponsor Caring Couple, pastor, and other Caring Couples about concerns and conflicts that typically arise in the initial months of marriage. In this way, the church's ministries through the Caring Couples Network Team can reach couples as issues first appear and can be more easily addressed.

The sponsor Caring Couple can also help the newlywed couple find marital counseling, professional consultation, and other resources they may need but not know how to find. The sponsor couple can encourage the newlywed couple to continue using the Caring Couples Network and other resources as needed.

Annual Marriage Enrichment Events

One goal of the Caring Couples Network Team is to sponsor annual marriage enrichment events. These events can be especially designed for newlywed couples or for all married couples (see Chapter 8). Couples can be encouraged to attend each year, and special discounts in costs might be arranged.

The sponsor Caring Couple can help the newlyweds connect with a church couples' class and with other available church groups. Newlywed couples with children may be assisted to participate in parenting training events and/or step-family parenting support groups.

Couples communication training can be available as part of "Celebrating Marriage" or in cooperation with "Marriage Encounter: United Methodist" (MEUM), A.C.M.E., or other resources. The enrichment and communication training events can be organized with groups of churches.

Congregations and Marriage

Appropriate recognition of newlywed couples among other couples on their marriage journey can be made by churches through a marriage celebration banquet, picnic, or other church activities at various times during the year. Caring Couples may give their own stories about marriage. This can also be a time to affirm the ministries of the Caring Couples Network Team.

Chapter 11
A Program for Reaching Parents

The Caring Couples Network Team can join with the existing worship, church school, and other local church efforts to implement the baptismal commitments outlined in Chapter 1. The team can assist families to find and utilize home worship resources such as the Bible, *The Upper Room, Alive Now, Pockets,* and other resources for reading Scripture, sharing stories and concerns, and prayer in the home.

Marriage and Parenting

The quality of parenting is related to the quality of the relationship between the parents and other caregivers. Most principles that apply to parents also apply to others (step-parents, relatives, child care workers, neighbors) who have important caregiving responsibilities with children.

Agreement and Openness of Parents

Parents need to agree to discuss changes in parenting policies and rules with each other before either parent agrees to make a change requested by the child. When the marriage relationship is healthy, open, and flexible, both parents can talk

with each other about child care without either parent feeling defensive, offended, or put-down. When the marriage is strained or dysfunctional, parents are vulnerable to being divided by a child seeking his or her own will.

Parental Consistency

Consistency in expressing love and affection and in applying parenting policies and rules to the child is essential for good parenting.

When one parent notices the other parent is inconsistent in following through on a disciplinary instruction, the parents need to find a time away from the child to talk about the matter. As parenting partners, spouses can agree on ways to review their parenting practices, gain information as needed, and support each other in parenting. A healthy marriage makes agreement possible. An unhealthy marriage prevents this from happening.

When a child thinks that parents are unfair or inconsistent, parents can invite the child to talk with them about how the situation should be changed. This strategy gives both parents and children opportunity to talk about situations and find constructive solutions. This avoids having rules arbitrarily imposed by parents. The family can modify goals, policies, and rules according to the growth and developmental stages of both children and parents.

The foundation of consistency is in the commitment of parents to be present and caring for each other and for their family members in all situations. When this does not happen, parents can model the way to examine the situation and find better answers. The assurance that parents love each other and love their children is always more important then having or not having answers to specific questions.

Parents as Models for Children to Imitate

As co-leaders in the family, parents can model fairness, respect, warmth, openness, commitment, and other Christian values. Children imitate those whom they perceive to have power in the family, which usually are the parents and other adults. Modeling includes enabling children to be aware of the consequences of their behavior as well as the behavior itself, even when consequences may come later.

Children are sensitive observers of their parents' marriage relationship. Out of these experiences children construct their own expectations and understandings of marriage, often dramatizing some of these in the ways they "play house" and treat siblings and friends. Parents are automatically models whose actions speak louder than their words. Marriage is the initial relationship in which spouses establish and modify habits of care and love.

Enabling Autonomy in Growing Children

Parenting moves from parents having total control and responsibility for their infant children to removing themselves completely from parental control of their young adult children. God's covenant encourages people to move from dependency to friendship with God in Christ (John 15:12–17; 1 John 4).

A major goal of good parenting is that parents work themselves out of parenting by gradually giving more independence to their children. A healthy marriage enables the spouses to move from being guardians to being friends to their adult children.

In a healthy marriage neither parent has to turn to the child (or children) to obtain the affirmation and support that spouses give each other throughout their marriage journey. Marriage is more than parenting; yet parents continue their love and concern for their children throughout life.

The Complexity of Step-Parenting

Step-families include all fundamental parenting dimensions, plus the additional issues that arise from the relationship of one or both parents to previous spouses or lovers.

In addition to the impact of the current marriage on parenting, step-families also have to cope with biological parents who may still be very emotionally involved with the children and/or have legal rights with the children. These relationships affect the parenting of the couple with whom the children are currently living.

Marriage affects many parenting, step-parenting, and other family concerns. The Caring Couples Network Team can identify specific parenting needs and means of ministry to these needs with available resources, time, and opportunities.

Important Transitional Contacts

Ministries with couples include parenting issues and concerns. The following suggestions may encourage the Caring Couples Network Team in creating ministry with parents of children at significant transitional stages.

Childbirth and Newborns

1. Caring Couples can visit a mother and father in the hospital or at home soon after delivery. Since hospital stays may be very short, a telephone call may need to substitute for a hospital visit. Having both members of the Caring Couple contact the new mother and father models the caring of both men and women for newborns and infants.

2. On behalf of the team (which should provide the materials), a Caring Couple can offer gifts to the family. These gifts may include a baby blanket, a booklet on newborns, and/or gifts for other children in the family who have a new brother or sister. Interested persons in the church could make baby blankets, puzzles, and/or other items to be given in the name of the church.

3. When the new baby is an additional child (not the first born to the couple), Caring Couples can be aware of the older children's needs. In step-families additional issues may be triggered if there are "his," "her," and now "our" children in the family.

4. The team may also minister with new mothers who have no one to help them when they come home from the hospital or cope with many other details that a baby requires. Since these women may have had fewer opportunities to experience healthy

couples, contacts with a caring couple can model positive marriage qualities.

5. Caring Couples could visit expectant parents during the latter stages of pregnancy and encourage them in appropriate ways.

Infancy and Early Childhood

1. A Caring Couple could offer care for children every two or three weeks while parents have an "evening out" for refreshment and renewal. Having a baby in the home is both exciting and exhausting. Too often couples with infants are forgotten after the initial days of congratulations. Caring Couples could extend this support for several months as needed by the parents.

2. According to the age of the Caring Couple, they can minister with the new parents somewhat like "grandparents" or "uncle/aunt" to the new parents and child. This may be especially important for couples who do not have relatives nearby or who may have negative or destructive relationships with relatives.

3. Caring Couples may assist parents with medical checkups, care, and other needs. This may be especially important when one parent must be away from the family for extended periods because of work or other requirements.

4. The team can review the nursery, nursery home visitor, and other local church services for young children. Often providing good quality child care for preschool children is a good way to help parents establish a current church relationship. When the church provides good child care along with classes for couples/parents, it demonstrates support for Christian families.

5. At baptism, Caring Couples can be "sponsors" (or "godparents") of infants and young children.

School Age and Later Childhood

1. The Caring Couples Network Team may help create and sponsor parenting classes at any stage of parenthood. These classes can also give attention to the ways in which marriage and parenting interact.

2. Many churches seek couples as co-teachers or sponsors of children's classes and events. Although individuals of both sexes are always needed, married couples provide models of marriage for growing children. When both spouses are involved in the leadership of children's activities, each partner can encourage the other in joint work that can bring them together in common activities.

3. Some churches award Bibles to children in the third or fourth grade. This could be an opportunity to help parents teach the use of the Bible in family devotions and encourage use of the Bible. Caring Couples who participate in the Disciple Bible study (or other Bible studies) could cooperate in providing models for Bible study.

4. Marriage enrichment retreats and events can be planned in cooperation with children's activities to answer both child care needs during the retreat as well as remind parents that they are still a caring couple.

5. Caring Couples may provide ministries to couples with chronic or long-term child-related conditions, such as disabilities caused by disease or accident. Some caring couples may themselves be coping with similar situations and can be especially helpful to other couples who are faced with these problems.

6. The Caring Couples Network Team can seek ways to minister to couples (usually late twenties through early forties) with older children. These couples are often caught by pressures from job demands, children's schooling, financial limitations, and the need to care for other family members or relatives.

7. The team can find ways to give hope and encouragement to parents of older children, since much research on marriage shows that marital satisfaction tends to be at its lowest ebb for couples who have older children. Important marriage transitions occur as the oldest child enters junior high, the youngest child enters first grade, and one or both parents make job, career, or education changes.

8. Healthy man-woman relationships need to be part of the programs for boys and girls through the various programs (Scouting, sports, etc.) that may focus on one sex. Middle and later childhood is typically the time when boys and girls prefer their own gender groups, yet need the healthy gender models that married couples can provide.

Parents of Adolescents and Young Adults

1. The Caring Couples Network Team can help parents of emerging adolescents obtain accurate information about sexuality, drugs, and other issues that adolescents face today.

2. Caring Couples may participate as sponsors in the youth ministries of their church.

3. The team can arrange for programs on family-related topics such as male-female friendships, dating, teenage marriage, and sexually-transmitted diseases. These may be offered through the church for junior high, high school, and college-age persons.

4. Parents of adolescents, typically late thirties through the fifties in age, are facing

their own mid-life transitions, community leadership opportunities and challenges, more intensive coping with their own aging parents, being at or beyond reaching their highest career and life goals, and other issues. Marriage enrichment events for these couples may be planned in cooperation with couples' classes and groups and can address issues which these couples face.

5. "Empty-nest" transitions may be seen as welcomed opportunities by some parents but as losses and disappointments by others. These may interact with long-term marital dysfunctions (see Chapter 12) that Caring Couples can address in friendship ministries with these couples.

6. Parents of college-age young adults may help support campus ministries and related college programs. The team may create ways for this support to be balanced with the need of young adults to be independent and away from their parents. Other parents may face the impact on marriage of having children who are too dependent to leave home.

Deciding the Caring Couples Network Team's Focus

A Caring Couples Network Team needs to decide to focus on parenting and marriage concerns. Each situation will be different. Caring Couples Network Teams are invited to recognize and minister to the many opportunities for marriage enrichment presented by parenting issues.

Chapter 12
Reaching Couples with Specific Needs

Caring Couples know what makes a good marriage. The key principles are expressed in very compact form by the six qualities of caring couples: Growing, Communicating, Negotiating, Renewing, Learning, and Reaching Out (see Chapters 3 and 5 and the *Caring Couples Network Video*).

Many couples, however, are not able to experience the joys, pleasures, and fulfillment that God intended marriage to provide. It is unlikely that any couple deliberately intends to be miserable, dysfunctional, or dissatisfied in their marriage. The brief classification that follows may help the local Caring Couples Network Team consider effective ways to minister with couples in their church and community.

Marriages can be classified on a broad spectrum from very healthy to very dysfunctional. These three categories point to ranges along this continuum.

- Healthy spouses needing enrichment, education, and support for marriage.
- Basically healthy couples facing unusual stressors.
- Couples with severe personal dysfunctions that destroy marriage.

Caring Couples have answers that couples need. At the least, team members may covenant to pray especially for couples in stressful situations. The goal of this chapter is to help local Caring Couples Network Teams design ministries to specific situations. Pastors and professional consultants may help teams refine these categories according to local needs.

Healthy Spouses Needing Enrichment, Education, and Support

The marriage enrichment resources described in Chapters 8–11 are designed to support basically healthy marriages. The ministries with engaged/newlywed couples and with parents as couples (Chapters 10–11) also generally assume that the spouses are spiritually and psychologically healthy, committed to God, and open to learning better ways to grow in love. This chapter seeks to sensitize Caring Couples Network Teams to more difficult and challenging situations.

Basically Healthy Couples Facing Unusual Stressors

Many couples face difficult situations that might be considered typical frustrations of living. The fragile spiritual and

CARING COUPLES NETWORK HANDBOOK

psychological health of each spouse, coupled with the severity of life pressures, will push some couples into the second category of marital functioning—couples facing unusual stress.

There are two general sources of marital strain:

- Events completely beyond the control of either spouse.
- Events controlled by the spouses.

Events Beyond the Control of Either Spouse

Some persons with supportive families and friends, healthy personalities, and high commitment to their own marriage may face severe crises and stress because of an accident, chronic illness, sudden change in economic conditions, death of a child, being a crime victim, or other factors beyond their direct control.

The distressful situation may be temporary or permanent. Some couples may cope well with one extra anxiety, yet need support when two or three crises hit them in succession. These couples may greatly benefit from caring couples who are coping constructively with similar experiences. Long-term couple-to-couple friendships may be a most effective way to minister with these couples.

Since there may be many couples in a church and community who are quietly suffering through major threats, the team may design specific events, consultations, and other programs to reach couples unknown to the pastor or team members.

Events Controlled by the Spouses

Some pressures may be controlled by the interactions between the spouses,

although the couple may not recognize the causes of these patterns. Among these may be occasional mildly abusive patterns; conflicts over money, sex, parenting, or other matters; one-time sexual misconduct of some type; or financial crises.

In these situations the spouses' capacity to recognize their contributions to the hurtful situation is a major determining factor for recovery. Marriage is a system in which the actions of each spouse set the stage for the other partner to respond, provoking counter responses and a chronic pattern of hurt, attack, and counter moves.

Sensitive Caring Couples can help couples find methods for coping with these events and recognizing both their contribution and their renewed commitment to change for the better. In designing ministries with these moderately dysfunctional couples, the Caring Couples Network Team can benefit by input from consultants about these situations as the team creates effective and healthy ministries to these couples.

Friendships with Caring Couples, especially those who have coped well with similar events in their own marriages, is a major ministry the team can offer to these couples. The team can help these couples find appropriate marital, family, and/or individual therapy as well as consultation with other professionals whose services can help.

Couples with Severe Personal Conditions that Destroy Marriage

This category includes all of the serious marital dysfunctions that usually require professional help. A major ministry by caring couples is to encourage the couple in need to seek help and to continue in outpatient or in-patient care long enough to address the issues sufficiently.

Marriage is stressful because it challenges partners to grow in love. Some persons function well in other life settings but are unable to relate well to one person in the intimacies of marriage over a long period of time.

Personality and Marriage

In general, persons tend to marry partners who are at somewhat the same personal development levels. Thus healthy persons can draw on many more personal resources to succeed in marriage. The same dynamic also is present for persons who have far fewer personal resources and skills for marriage. Surface attractions may initially bring them together, but the challenges of daily living may trigger ever more hurtful and harmful patterns in their marriage until divorce, desertion, or even murder interrupts the cycle.

A major challenge to Caring Couples Network Teams is to find ways to minister with these more chronically dysfunctional couples. They also are our neighbors in Christ, for whom Christ cares and whom God continues to seek in love. In human terms, however, they may be the most difficult and least attractive for caring couple outreach ministries.

The Caring Couples Network Team may consider how it can minister to these challenging situations:

- Alcohol abuse and/or other drug dependent couples.
- Emotional, physical, and/or sexual abuse by one spouse of the other spouse.
- Child abuse by one or both parents.
- Neglect of spouse, children, and home.
- Mental illness conditions, both organic and functional, such as major depression, schizophrenia, personality dysfunctions, and character disorders.
- Addictions such as gambling, sexual affairs, and perversions.
- Felony offense and imprisonment.
- Distortions and misuse of religion, education, or other areas of human life that imprison, manipulate, or control one's spouse and/or children.
- Changing health conditions of one spouse that affect the marriage relationship.

These conditions require well-trained and competent professional treatment that is usually beyond the scope of most caring couples and pastors. Parallel with such treatment, however, the team can provide a very valuable ministry of friendship, information, and encouragement to these more dysfunctional couples.

In deciding on these aspects of Caring Couples Network Team ministry, a team may use professional consultants who have experience working with specific types of couples. A Caring Couples Network Team's decision to become involved in these ministries may relate to whether it has Caring Couples who are coping well with similar situations and are willing to volunteer as Caring Couples with these more seriously dysfunctional couples.

Chapter 13
Reaching One-Parent Families, Widowed, Divorced, and Other Non-Couple Situations

The primary emphasis of the Caring Couples Network is on strengthening engaged and married couples, but other family situations are also of concern to the network. Post-marriage situations result from the death of a spouse or divorce. There are also situations that might be termed "quasi-marriage," such as couples living together with no intention of getting married. The Caring Couples Network Team may want to consider these situations as part of its ministry.

"Couples" or "Marriages"

In some areas there is reaction to the term "marriage" and a tendency to reduce the significance of marriage by substituting "couple" for "marriage," as in "couple therapy." This issue was considered in naming the ministry of married couples the "Caring Couples Network." The term "Couples" in the Caring Couples Network name means married couples ministering to couples who are engaged or married or struggling with marriage relationship issues.

At times a genuine concern for non-married adults has caused churches to reduce celebration of healthy, intact marriages. They fear that persons who are not married will feel excluded when special notice of married couples is made in wor-

ship, programming, or other church ministries. The clear emphasis of the Caring Couples Network is providing ministries by married couples to couple, marriage, and family situations selected by the team.

Toward a Balanced View

Because of the Caring Couples Network's concern for Christian marriage as the intentional and public foundation for the family, this handbook may seem to indicate that the Caring Couples Network proposes that marriage is the primary means to relational health. This is not so. It is true that deep commitment to Christian marriages and families gives clear focus to ministries that enable healthy marriages. The network organizers also hope, however, that others will develop ministries to situations that are outside the Caring Couples Network focus.

The Caring Couples Network Team needs to engage in open discussion of these concerns. The team must carefully consider how to minister in situations that do not involve engaged or married couples.

Examples of Ministries in Non-Couple Situations

Because there are other ministries to non-couples, the Caring Couples Network

Team can offer some unique contributions to non-couple situations. The ministries of caring couples can meet needs from a unique perspective.

Advantages to the Persons Receiving Caring Couple Ministries

- Caring Couples model in everyday life how a woman and a man can make Christian marriage work.
- Caring Couples bring both a male and a female perspective to situations.
- The Caring Couples Network Team may be able to stimulate, encourage, and support other existing ministries to single parents and other non-couple situations.
- In some situations a married couple can give an increased sense of safety to those receiving a ministry.
- Where contacts are made as a couple, neither the recipient of ministry nor others can accuse the caring couple of trying to misuse the ministry for sexual purposes.

Advantages to the Caring Couple Providing Ministries

- The spouses in a Caring Couple provide support for each other as they work together ministering to others.
- The perspectives of each spouse on a ministry situation can help both to identify the most effective ways to minister. It can keep both spouses from becoming inappropriately dependent on the others involved for emotional gratification.
- A Caring Couple can discuss the non-couple situation and have more ministry options than either may have alone.

- The Caring Couple can learn from those whom they seek to serve. This may impact the ways the Caring Couple serves, how they allocate their own resources, and their awareness of and ideas for needed services.

Caring Couple Experiences in Relation to Specific Circumstances

- A Caring Couple with one or both partners having been previously widowed may be better able to help a widowed person think through such concerns as remarriage, allegiance to the deceased spouse, family concerns, and financial arrangements.
- A Caring Couple with one or both spouses previously divorced may help a divorced person identify more accurately his or her own contributions to the divorce and the need for personal growth and therapy.
- In the case of one-parent situations arising from divorce or death, a Caring Couple may help to include the individual comfortably in mixed couple and individual classes, social events, and church activities.
- In the case of one-parent situations where the parent was never married and the child was intentionally conceived or adopted, a Caring Couple may model a healthy marriage and help the individual to address deeper issues that caused him or her to avoid marriage and the challenges it brings.
- In one-parent family situations, the Caring Couple may model healthy marriage for the children, especially if the parent does not have many married friends or friends of the other sex.

Chapter 14
Connecting the Caring Couples Network to the Ministries of the Congregation

The Caring Couples Network is a ministry of The United Methodist Church to couples and families, implemented through Caring Couples Network Teams in every local church. The Caring Couples Network Team must be officially recognized as a church's ministry by having a clear place in the church's administrative structure with money allocated for the team's work.

The Caring Couples Network Team is related to other local church ministries and focuses on marriages and family ministries without overlapping with other structures. The Caring Couples Network Team should be connected with the local congregation's administrative structures, pastoral care plan, and discipleship ministries.

The Caring Couples Network and Administrative Structures

The Caring Couples Network should be established and approved as part of the church's ministry by the appropriate administrative body of the local church. This may be the Church Council, Council on Ministries, Administrative Board, or Administrative Council.

By setting reporting and accountability structures, the Administrative Board and the pastor affirm and authorize the Caring Couples Network Team. Endorsement by the official leadership is essential for the team to join the church's cooperative ministries.

The Administrative Board or Church Council

Funding for the Caring Couples Network Team should be provided in the church budget in ways similar to funding for ministries to children, youth, adults, and other groups.

The Caring Couples Network Team line item in the church budget needs to include funding for purchasing Caring Couples Network materials, training of team members, conducting enrichment events, providing information, and supplies.

The pastor and the Administrative Board can decide how the Caring Couples Network Team will be accountable to the congregation through the organizational structure of the local church. The Caring Couples Network Team should be related to the administrative unit that is responsible for pastoral and educational ministries of the church.

The Council on Ministries

One Caring Couple should be named to represent the Caring Couples Network Team on the Council on Ministries (or equivalent unit) so the local church can view the team's ministries in relation to other ministries of the congregation. This council should recommend funding for the team and general responsibilities that the team will assume.

The reports of the Caring Couples Network Team to the Council on Ministries may describe the team's work without disclosing confidential information about specific families. Included in the regular reports may be names of Caring Couples teams and consultants, the number of couples and families that have received ministries from the team, results of training and enrichment events, and recommendations about ministry needs known to the team.

The Caring Couples Network Team reports should never disclose information about Partner Couples without specific permission from the persons involved. In confidential Caring Couples Network Team meetings and contacts, the pastor, Caring Couples, and consultants may discuss details that are essential for the team's ministry, but these discussions are not part of any report.

The Council on Ministries can facilitate the work of the Caring Couples Network Team through interpreting its work and supporting it in relation to budget needs, publicity, scheduling, and other aspects of the work of the local church.

The Family Life Committee

If your church has a Family Life Committee or other nurture committee, the Caring Couples Network Team may be part of the work of this committee and relate to the Council on Ministries through it.

The Caring Couples Network supports healthy family relationships. The network's approach to family life may fit with other committee goals or may deserve its own equivalent committee.

The Caring Couples Network Team and Pastoral Care

The Caring Couples Network Team ministries fall primarily into the pastoral care, discipleship, and evangelistic outreach efforts of the local church. Regardless of where the team is placed in the church's administrative structure, it is vital for the Caring Couples Network Team to be related to these local church ministries.

- The pastor can call on the Caring Couples Network Team for ministries to couples and families with need as an extension of pastoral care in the parish and community.
- *The Caring Couples Network Video* may be used in program presentations to local church groups.

The church's care for the institutions of marriage and family is eminently pastoral. This pastoral care for marriages is expressed in all of the ministries suggested in this *Caring Couples Network Handbook*. The pastoral opportunities surrounding the wedding are in the context of the shepherding care for couples and families in the congregation.

Lay Counseling and Other Pastoral Care Expressions

If a church has a lay counseling program or other pastoral care program, Caring

Couples may receive additional training through these resources. However, the Caring Couples Network is not the same as lay counseling, since Caring Couples Network Teams provide friendship and support while lay counselors are trained to provide counseling under professional supervision.

The Caring Couples Network Team should be clearly related to the other pastoral care structures of the local church.

The Caring Couples Network Team and Discipleship

Ministries with couples and families involve nurture, education, discipleship, and spiritual formation. The Caring Couples Network Team may:

- Work with adult classes, study groups, or fellowship groups in the church.
- Lift up the full range of family ministries in the local church.
- Relate to the women's and the men's organizations of the local church.
- Assist in organizing couples' classes and educational opportunities for couples.
- Co-sponsor marriage and family events with adult classes and other groups.

In these ways teams cooperate with the pastor and church leaders to increase the quality of the church's ministry to couples, marriages, and families through marriage enrichment, parenting classes, and other programs and services.

Caring concern and outreach to couples who are not actively related to the congregation is an expression of evangelistic witness. While the primary mission of Caring Couples Network Teams is not to get couples to join the church, caring support and nurture encourage couples and families to become connected with others who value home and family.

Caring Couples witness to the ways that God is involved in their own lives as they seek to reach families. Through friendships, examples, and words, Caring Couples Network Teams proclaim God's love for all persons. Professing their own faith in Christ and joining other Christians can become a basic foundation which motivates couples and families to grow.

Telling Others about Caring Couples Network Team Ministries

- Caring Couples Network ministries may be highlighted through occasional presentations and parish announcements in worship services.
- Teams may encourage the congregation to pray regularly for the ministries of the Caring Couples Network.
- The congregation and leaders can be enabled to view Caring Couple ministries as equally important with children, youth, education, and discipleship in the local church.
- Christian marriage may be lifted up through a church event around Valentine's Day, Mother's Day, Father's Day, the Festival of the Christian Home, or other seasons.
- Caring Couples may be invited to describe their work as part of a worship service, fellowship night, or other all-church settings.
- Articles about Caring Couples Network and Christian marriage can be published in the church bulletin, newspaper, and other materials for the congregation.